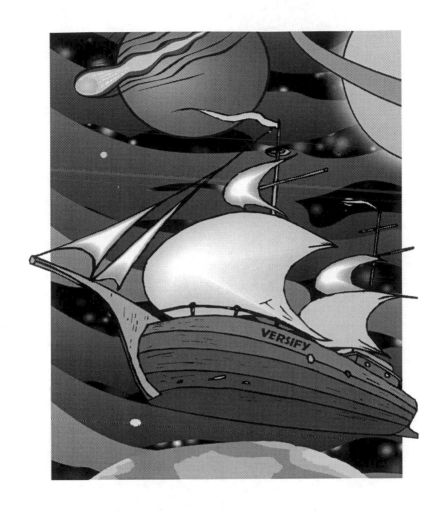

POETIC VOYAGES
MIDDLESEX VOL II

Edited by Donna Samworth

First published in Great Britain in 2002 by
YOUNG WRITERS
Remus House,
Coltsfoot Drive,
Peterborough, PE2 9JX
Telephone (01733) 890066

HB ISBN 0 75433 428 7
SB ISBN 0 75433 429 5

FOREWORD

Young Writers was established in 1991 with the aim to promote creative writing in children, to make reading and writing poetry fun.

This year once again, proved to be a tremendous success with over 88,000 entries received nationwide.

The Poetic Voyages competition has shown us the high standard of work and effort that children are capable of today. It is a reflection of the teaching skills in schools, the enthusiasm and creativity they have injected into their pupils shines clearly within this anthology.

The task of selecting poems was therefore a difficult one but nevertheless, an enjoyable experience. We hope you are as pleased with the final selection in *Poetic Voyages Middlesex Vol II* as we are.

CONTENTS

Edgware Junior School

Holland House School

Rosh Pinah Primary School

The Poems

JAWS THE SHARK

Jaws the shark,
Lived in the Pacific Ocean.
His long, sharp teeth scared anyone near him,
Because he was a silent *hunter.*
He was a mean, vindictive creature.
He ate little fish and humans.
He lived in a mean group of seven.
Never had he done any good,
But once, he killed an innocent two year old,
And finally, I chose him because he is fascinating.

Priyan Patel (10)
Alpha Preparatory School

THE LION

The lion is the king of beasts, a Leo.
Lives in his den in his jungle in India.
He has orange brown fur and a furry, furry mane.
Roar, roar, roaring fiercely.
Vindictive, fierce, clever.
He attacks his prey, jumping fast.
The lion brings his small family food to share.
He protects them from all their enemies.
But he attacks and kills.
The lion is interesting and fun to learn about.

Krissma Ladwa (10)
Alpha Preparatory School

THE BLOOD HUNTER

A grown-up tiger is known as a striped devil
Comes from Africa and lives in my garden
Ferocious black and orange striped
Roar! Roar! Roar!
Ferocious and trustworthy
Eats dead meat smothered in blood
His mum is kind-hearted
His dad is reckless and terrifying
Excretes on the bullies
Comes into school and chews the football
at break which causes lots of trouble.
I chose the animal because it's my favourite animal
And I like its attitude.

Jamie Everitt (10)
Alpha Preparatory School

LITTLE LOVE BIRD

My pet is a budgie,
It lives in a cage which is cosy like a buggy!
It is blue and slimy and has small beady eyes,
It goes cheep, cheep, cheep and sounds like it cries,
It bites if you touch him, otherwise he's good.
If you don't mention that, he's not in a bad mood.
He stays with a tall thin mother and her caring family.
If you tell him off he'll cry and do a wee!
I chose this bird because he's really cute.
But sometimes at least once in a week I wish he would mute.

Chandni Sodha (10)
Alpha Preparatory School

KERRY - THE PUP

Kerry the pup my pride and joy.
She lives in my house the friendly thing.
She's cute and sweet and she's man's best friend
But!
Kerry whimpers a lot and she can be a pain,
She eats dog food and she's a human vacuum cleaner.
We are her family and we love her to death.
And to protect us is her first intent.
Though if she bites that's the worst she can do.
So she says she's sorry and that's the right thing to do.
We wanted a dog so we got her and to give a dog
        a loving home.

Jodi Richardson (9)
Alpha Preparatory School

THE LITTLE BABY FOX

The little baby fox
Lives in the dark, dark earth.
It's small and red and its tail flaps behind.
It whines and cries for its mother when it's alone.
It's small friendly and sweet.
It feeds on milk from mother and meat from rabbits.
His father is vicious and his mother is kind.
He is small but doesn't do evil things.
But he eats animals his father kills.
I like baby foxes because they are cute.

Ramiyya Rajah (10)
Alpha Preparatory School

THE KING OF BEASTS

The king of beasts, Leo the lion
Lives in the zoo in England
Roar! Roar! *Roar!*
Grand, strong, proud and loyal
Vicious, violent and unfriendly.
Eats the meat of zebra and deer
Friendly family but always cruel to him.
Whenever its family are hungry it goes out
And gets food for them.
But whenever his family are nice to him
It makes a horrid noise.
I've chosen this animal because it's vicious,
Huge and'll eat you
'Ha, ha, ha.'

Amish Parekh (10)
Alpha Preparatory School

THE LION

Leo the lion, big and scary
All the way from Africa
Its mane so long and looks fierce
Roar, roar, roar! He goes all day
He's one of the best friends you can ever have
Give him food, watch him gobble it
The only family it has is us
Scares away all of the robbers
But sometimes scares away friends.
Cutest animal in the world.

Maryam Saleh (9)
Alpha Preparatory School

MOANING FELIX

Orang-utan with the name of Felix
Lives in the trees by himself.
Scared and when angry very powerful
Makes moaning noises all the time.
Shows power when helping those in trouble
Always eats leaves, bananas, grapes and oranges.
Is a real loner.
He protects things that are in danger.
When he gets angry he will hurt you badly
I chose this because there is a monkey in a film I like.

Harveer Bhalla (9)
Alpha Preparatory School

ODDBALL THE DALMATIAN

Oddball, Oddball you naughty Dalmatian
You live at my house as a pain.
You're spotty, cute and small.
Woof, woof, woof, bark, bark, bark.
Friendly smart cute.
Yum coco mmm biscuits you like meat.
We are your family.
Good girl where's Mum's bracelet?
I chose this because you're cute.

Francesca Dunworth (9)
Alpha Preparatory School

RAINBOW STONES

Red is for a garnet gleaming like the brightest sunset
With the shine of a star in the middle.
Orange is a topaz a sweet and pretty stone
The orange gleams bright and clear.
Yellow is gold with sparks of sunlight
Like the stars.

Green is an emerald as green as grass
Shining brilliantly in the sun
Blue is sapphire as deep as the blue sea
Which goes up the shore.

Indigo is an amethyst the indigo diamond
A magnificent glow as well
Violet is a frost gleam, one of the many colours in an opal.

Charlotte Calderwood-Hart (9)
Ashford CE Primary School

THE VOYAGE OF LIFE

He is riding out the storm,
The greatest storm of all.
Lightning flashing, here and there and everywhere.
Trying to sail to a distant land, far, far away.
The sea is rough, very rough.
Up and down goes the boat.
It feels like a very little piece of wood.
Just a small, small plank of wood.
Will it reach its destination?

Maria Metzger (9)
Ashford CE Primary School

RAINBOW LIGHTS

Red is for the elegant rose spreading out its petals,
And making its fragrance flow.
Orange is for the trumpet of the daffodil, swaying in the
Moonlit breeze.
Yellow is for corn, a golden relaxing colour
Green is an apple shiny with light.
Blue is for sapphire, dug out with care,
An enlightening thing, with its daintiness and light.
Indigo is a plum, a juicy round ball a juice we all love.
Violet is pansies, a wonderful colour,
It brightens our day in rain or storm.
And these are the colours of the rainbow.

Jennifer Frost (9)
Ashford CE Primary School

ALL THE COLOURS OF THE RAINBOW

Red is for red rosy apples, swaying in the trees.
Orange is for fire, flaming in the breeze.
Yellow is for daffodils, dancing in the wind.
Green is for emerald, flashing in the sun.
Blue is for blue tits, flying in the moonlit sky.
Indigo is for plums, juicy and sweet.
Violet is for liquorice sweet, chewy like meat.
They're all the colours of the rainbow.

Louise Read (8)
Ashford CE Primary School

THE INCREDIBLE COLOURS OF THE RAINBOW

Red is for lips as beautiful as a ruby
Soft and gentle to kiss, a young child.
Orange is for a marigold swaying in the lovely breeze
They make me feel happy when I'm sad.
Yellow is the sun in the sky, shining down on the
sandy beach below.

Green is for an emerald shining when the sun gleams on it.
Blue is for a blue tit swaying its wings in the breeze and
singing happily.

Indigo is for an amethyst in a nice, big, gold necklace for a lady in a
nice big gold necklace
Violet is for a plum as sweet as a sweet with a violet taste
in your mouth.

Anthony Bradley (9)
Ashford CE Primary School

THE RAINBOW COLOURS

Red is for roses, so sweet as love,
Orange is for sunset, so dark and cool,
Yellow is for lemon, so juicy and so sweet,
Green is for caterpillar, slow and slimy,
Blue is for blue tit, flapping its wings,
Indigo is for grapes, lots of them in Britain.
Violet is for plum, juicy all through, hey you should love it!

Ashley Gadd (8)
Ashford CE Primary School

EVERYDAY LIFE OF THE RAINBOW COLOURS

Red is a strawberry as sweet as sugar,
A treat on a summer's day.
Orange is as hot as flames, that will always
Be in your heart.
Yellow is a pineapple, as sour as lemons,
Lions are the fiercest, but a daffodil is the sweetest.

Green is an emerald nice to look at too,
But melon is quite sweet but grapes are even sweeter.

Blue is like the sky, while sapphire is very expensive
But Topaz is even more expensive.
Indigo is the violet but quite different colours they are.
Violet is like a grape because it looks nice, smells nice
and tastes nice.

George Ingham (8)
Ashford CE Primary School

RAINBOW SURPRISES

Red is for strawberries, nice and sweet.
Orange is for flames shooting up.
Yellow is for sunflower shining in the sun
Green is for grass glittering with green.
Blue is for blue tits flying around
Indigo is for grapes tasty for all
Violet is for pansies fragrant and nice.

Faye Sibley (8)
Ashford CE Primary School

THE COLOURS OF THE RAINBOW

Red is for roses sweet as pure perfume
Which is spreading in the world.
Orange is for the sunset blazing in the sky,
Making morning light.
Yellow is for daffodil, the sweet smelling flowers,
Makes people happy especially me too.

Green is for grass shining underneath our feet,
Brightening our world.
Blue is for the sea roaring up and down
Sometimes maybe floods.

Indigo is for grapes, lots of them in Britain.
I love the taste.
Violet is for plum, fresh fruit too.
The cover is velvety, it is juicy all through.

John Kim (8)
Ashford CE Primary School

THE COLOURS OF THE RAINBOW

Red is for robins that sing in the air,
So sweet and loving in the breeze.
Orange is for a tiger that purrs in the grass.
Yellow is for the sand, gold in the sun
And at the water's edge.

Green is for leaves that sway in the breeze.
Blue is for the sea, waves spray in the air.

Indigo is for grapes that hang on branches.
Violet is for a butterfly that flies in the air.

Amy Burge (9)
Ashford CE Primary School

THE COLOUR OF THE RAINBOW

Red is for roses that shine all the time
Bringing delight in gardens.
Orange is for fire that you light at a camp
And sit around.
Yellow is for sun, as bright as can be,
You loll in the summer sun.

Green is for apples, that fall off trees,
And arc as crunchy as can be.
Blue is for the sea, you see big waves,
The salt water and the huge tides on the sea.

Indigo is for grapes that you can eat,
Very juicy and as fresh as can be.
Violet is for violet that is the last colour of the rainbow.

Karl Yates (9)
Ashford CE Primary School

THE AMAZING COLOUR

Red is for ruby that shines through the night.
Orange is for sunset that shines in my eyes.
Yellow is for ducklings that quacks all day long.

Green is for bushes that squish fast
Blue is for blueberry that is sweet as sweets.

Indigo is for grapes that is crunchy as can be.
Violet is the last colour of the rainbow.

Danny Nicholls (8)
Ashford CE Primary School

THE COLOURS OF THE RAINBOW

Red is for roses that shine in the sunset,
A strawberry, all beautiful and sweet.
Orange as juicy as the fruit itself,
And as dangerous as a tiger so fierce.

Yellow so bright as the sun on the beach
To relax and feel the tiny grains of sand falling
                              through your hand.
Green apples as shiny as emeralds,
And the crunching of leaves being eaten by caterpillars.
Blue is beautiful to a blue tit,
And the sea is as blue as the light blue sky.

Indigo is as colourful as pansies,
And indigo smells of wonderful perfume that fills the air.
Violet is as purple as plums and as sweet as grapes,
And most important of all it is the last colour of the rainbow
Which wraps up my rainbow poem.

Matthew Wilkins (9)
Ashford CE Primary School

THE PRECIOUS THINGS OF THE RAINBOW

Red is for a heart you can have as a token of love
Orange is for a bright beautiful fire
Yellow for a gleaming moon in the dark night.

Green is for a lovely emerald in the sun.
Blue is for a magical sapphire to give to my love.

Indigo is for a pansy for a special gift.
Violet is for amethysts in a precious necklace.

Kirsty Hull (8)
Ashford CE Primary School

RAINBOW COLOURS

Red is for roses that all the petals fly off into the air.
The apples going away by the mouths.
Orange is for sunset that rises early every morning.
The fires flaming by the fireplace.
The ducks beak quacking on the pond.
Yellow sun coming towards us getting brighter and brighter,
It's as bright as some sugar.

Green grass blowing by the wind so the grass waves and waves.
Blue sky in the air where the clouds are and the lightning and
The sun and most of all God.
Indigo plums, getting all the lovely juice out of the plum
Eating all the purply skin after that.
Violet grapes crunching and crumbling.
The pansy almost in the air.
That's the colours of the rainbows.

Ryan Kerswill-Bennett (8)
Ashford CE Primary School

THE BEAUTIFUL COLOURS OF THE RAINBOW

R is red loving lips, so children can kiss you softly.
O is for oranges so lovely and fresh oranges,
So you can eat them.
Y is for yellow, yellow daffodils,
So your garden can be beautiful.

G is for green, green grass so you can walk on it.
B is for blue, a fresh blueberry to eat.

I is for indigo grapes, so lovely and fresh.
V is for violet, lovely fresh plums, so lovely and soft.

Nathan Yates (9)
Ashford CE Primary School

RAINBOW COLOURS

Red is for roses that sway in the wind,
And glow in the dark park at night.
Orange is for fire flames sparkling in the night
They make you feel all warm and cosy.
Yellow is for buttercups that open in the summer,
That shine at night-time and shine in the daytime
Like a buttercup should.

Green is for crunchy leaves that fall off the tree in autumn
They grow back on in the summer and never get stopped.
Blue is for bluebells that are lovely blue flowers
They sparkle in the day and night
Like a lovely flower always should.

Indigo is for grapes that grow on violets and are juicy to eat.
Violet is for juicy plums which are nice and big to eat
When you're hungry it is a big treat.

Georgina Solly (8)
Ashford CE Primary School

RAINBOW FLOWERS

Red is for the sugary sweetness in the lovely strawberry
That sways in the wind.
Orange is for sunset glistening, setting in the west.
Yellow is for buttercup that's opening its petals
Letting the fragrance flow.

Green is for emeralds shining in the light that twinkles in delight.
Blue often twinkling in the sunlight, you see just blue sea.
Indigo is for lovely sweet plums dangling in the breeze.
Violet is for violets that don't mind if it is sun, wind or rain.

Emma Sperling (8)
Ashford CE Primary School

Rainbow Colours

Red is for rose, beautiful and royal.
Red is for ruby that's so shiny it glows.
Orange is for sunset all glowing and red.
Orange is for trumpets leading the band.
Yellow is for bananas as yellow as paint
Yellow is for a duck going quack, quack.

Green is for weed growing in the grass
Green is for caterpillar eating some leaves.

Blue is for berry ready to eat
Blue is for sea shimmering and shining
Indigo is for the last colour of a rainbow
                A special colour this.
Violet is for violets, but this is my favourite colour.

Peter Buckmaster (9)
Ashford CE Primary School

Rainbow

Red is a rose sweet as love's soft velvet petals
And sweet strawberry hearts.
Orange a marigold swaying in the wind,
Tigers asleep in the beautiful sunset.
Yellow is a newborn chick what sits under the sun.

Green is apples with a sweet tasty taste
Emeralds sparkling in the moonlight.
Blue tits in the woods, wonderful blueberries,
Wave in the sea.
Indigo grapes yum, yum, yum lovely violets,
Violet pansies and a sweet cherry plum.

Becky Flatt (9)
Ashford CE Primary School

ANIMALS

Edward the echidna has a very long nose,
he uses it to sniff for food as he goes.

Kevin the koala climbs lots of trees,
while he's up there he eats lots of leaves.

Jennifer the giraffe is very tall
If she trips over she would have a hard fall.

Anthony antelope gallops around,
While Peter the pangolin sniffs the ground.

Robbie the rabbit jumps and sings
I love all of these wonderful things.

Shaun Newport (8)
Ashford CE Primary School

RAINBOW COLOURS

Red rosy apples swing on the beautiful trees.
Orange fire, flaming on a bonfire.
Yellow corn swaying in the sun, they look gold.

Green grass in the sun see them sway in the wind.
Blue stands for bluebells lovely and blue
If you pick which would be the one for you?

Indigo plums lovely and sweet,
Why don't you pick one for you to eat?
Violet is for crocuses swaying in the sun.

Rebecca Bogie (9)
Ashford CE Primary School

My Point Of View Of The Rainbow

Red as a rose also a sunset that makes me feel
In such a coat of plummet.
Orange as a marigold I'm never blue when I see a hullabaloo.
Yellow as a daffodil when the sun goes down
We call it sunset hot as fire.

Green's my favourite colour, it sparkles in the sun.
Blue as the sky as colourful as can be.

Indigo is pure, the best class of all,
It even makes me feel I have a wonderful deal.
Violet makes me sad, I feel blue when someone says boo,
But that's my point of view.

Jordan Cochrane (8)
Ashford CE Primary School

It's Snowing

It was snowing outside my window
Little snowflakes on the ground.
It is good that I am inside my bed
With a big pillow under my head.
There is a robin by the window
With its sharp pointed beak and redbreast.
It likes to eat seeds but berries are best.
It's time to go to sleep now
But first I must pray,
I am inside my cosy bed ready to sleep,
Ready to wake up on a new snowy day.

Joey Jennings (8)
Ashford CE Primary School

THE LIVE SNOWMAN

There was a snowman
All cold and white.
He was shiny and bright.

His nose was a carrot
All long and orange.
He had buttons for eyes,
And a hat all in black.

He sits and watches the children
Having fun making snowballs.
The sun turns up.
Turning, burning,
And he melted away
Never seen again.

Charlotte Ross (8)
Ashford CE Primary School

IF I WERE . . .

If I were a whale I'd live in the sea,
And have lots of lovely fish for tea.

If I were a cat I'd live in a house,
And for lunch I'd have a big fat mouse.

If I were a rabbit I'd live in a hutch,
And run around but not eat much.

If I were a dog I'd be man's best friend,
And look after him until the end.

Lauren Anthony (7)
Ashford CE Primary School

MY BIKE

When I'm on my bike
It gave me quite a fright
The wind is my enemy
I fall off my bike.

I graze my knee and chin
I wish I had gone in.
I shout for my mummy
Who came running.

She puts a plaster on my knee
I feel like normal me.
I don't think I will go on my bike
Instead I will get myself a trike.

Sasha Johal (8)
Ashford CE Primary School

NIBBLES

I have a little hamster
He's lovely golden brown
And when I take him out of his cage
He runs around and round.

My hamster's name is Nibbles,
He's small and fat and round
And when he gets out from his cage
He never can be found.

My hamster's very lively
He runs round in his ball
Nibbles is my best friend
I love him most of all.

Cathryn Quail (7)
Ashford CE Primary School

ROLLERBLADING

Rolling, rolling down the street,
Rollerblading is really neat.
Jumping high, learning tricks,
Making ramps, going quick.
Going places really fast.
Racing friends I'm never last.
Doing jumps I sometimes fall.
It doesn't hurt much at all.
I sometimes fall and rip my clothes,
Once I even cut my nose
I like rollerblading a real lot.
It makes me feel really hot.
When I come in from the street,
Mum always says 'Wipe your feet!'

Curtis Griffiths (7)
Ashford CE Primary School

THE BEST RUGBY DAY IN MY LIFE

I woke up on a very special day.
I went downstairs with my dressing gown on.
And had eggs and bacon.
I went to rugby in my daddy's car because it was not far.
When I got to rugby I saw Pierce who was muddy.
Then we both got grubby.
Then my friends came and we played a rugby game.
Then I scored a 'Try' and hurt my thigh.
I won a medal and everyone cheered.
This is the best rugby day for years.

Ben Lang (7)
Ashford CE Primary School

Rainbow Poem

Red is a silk rose swaying in the light breeze
Staining the air with a magnificent scent.
Orange is a candle that burns and flickers
In the pitch black night.
Yellow is a buttercup as yellow as the sun,
Growing in an open meadow swaying to and fro.

Green is the grass in an open meadow
Moving in the breeze.
Blue is a sapphire,
A glorious sight found underground sparkling bright.

Indigo is a pansy growing in the earth,
Fed on light, seen with delight.
Violet is a flower ever so sweet,
Pretty in a posy a lady's treat.

James Diamond (8)
Ashford CE Primary School

The Dinosaur

I bumped into a dinosaur on my way to school
He had big white teeth.
I hesitated for a little then got my courage back.
I bumped into a dinosaur on my way to school
I tried to make friends with him but all he did was roar.
I thought he was a rude dinosaur, on my way to school.

Oliver Parsons (8)
Ashford CE Primary School

I LOVE THIS GAME

I love this game of basketball
I play it every day
I like my school but even so
I can't wait to get away.

I do not like the winter
It's too cold to play outside
The summer is best because
I can shoot in my drive.

Number eight has always been
The number that I choose
My brother plays in this as well
We never like to lose.

I'm not tall enough
To slam dunk yet
I need to be at least six foot
To get it in the net.

I like to shoot
It's my favourite thing
To swish it through the hoop
And hear the crowd sing.

Thomas Morland (8)
Ashford CE Primary School

THE SHARK

See the monster big and grey
Swimming in circles around the bay
Teeth are big, eyes are dark
He's not your friend, or mine, he is the shark.

His fin in the air reaching the sky
He likes it that way, we don't ask why.
Time for some dinner, he may choose a fish
No knife, no fork, not even a dish.

Jakob McGillivray (8)
Ashford CE Primary School

RAINBOW POEM

Red is as red as a Valentine's rose,
Soft and silky.

Orange is a sunset,
Blazing really bright.

Yellow is the brightest sun,
Shimmering and sparkly.

Green is the fresh new grass,
Dancing in the wind.

Blue is the bluest sky
In midday.

Indigo is a butterfly,
Fluttering in the sky.

Violet is the colour of fresh new grapes,
Good enough to eat.

Megan McVey (9)
Ashford CE Primary School

RAINBOW POEM

Red is the colour of a Valentine heart,
Shiny, soft and as blood.

Orange is a tangerine,
Round, fat and juicy.

Yellow is a rubber ball,
Shiny, bright and bouncy.

Green is the colour of a set of fresh grass,
Swaying in the meadow.

Blue is a deep blue ocean
Splashing and hitting the cliff.

Indigo is a pansy,
Soft, thin and smelly,

Violet is the colour of a jumper,
Warm, soft and itchy.

Stephanie Ward (9)
Ashford CE Primary School

RAINBOW COLOURS

Red cheeks like a rose
Orange squash makes me happy
Yellow chicks peck all day
Green grapes are my favourite fruit
Blue sea makes me sick
Indigo comes from a plant
But violet is a plant I love.

Sophie Knight (9)
Ashford CE Primary School

RAINBOW POEM

Red is the colour of a shining Valentine heart,
If you stroke it your hand suddenly feels soft.

Orange is a ginger cat crawling through the grass,
Its fur is silky and velvety.

Yellow is the blazing sun that shines on a summer day,
And turns your skin copper.

Green is the colour of the pines on a pine tree
That prick you if you poke them.

Blue is the deep, dark ocean that sometimes looks grey.

Indigo is a drink that my nan buys,
It also tastes of apple.

Violet is a flower in forests,
It smells sweet and good enough to eat.

Jessica Naish (9)
Ashford CE Primary School

THE GREAT FOOTBALL DAY

I played football again
In the light rain.
Seven of us all
Chasing the ball.
I made a quick pass
As Joe ran fast.
They made an attack
As I hurried back.
But all was in vain
As defender is my name.

Jack Mayger (8)
Ashford CE Primary School

THE WHIZZING CAR

The car is fast
It whizzes past
The wheels go round
Without a sound.

It can be red or blue
And yellow too.
Any colour you like
Be careful to not hit a bike.

Do not drive off a cliff, you could take a big fall
But most important of all
Put on a seat belt
And you won't be hurt at all . . .

Robert Carty (8)
Ashford CE Primary School

THE HOLIDAY

We are going on holiday in the car
We have to travel so very far
We are looking forward to having fun
We are waiting very patiently for the sun
We want to go to the pool
When we get there the water is cool
We have made a new friend called Mike
He has got a very cool bike
We've had a great day
And I want to play another day.

Sarah Biffen (7)
Ashford CE Primary School

THE SEASONS

The sun is yellow and spring is here.
The flowers grow this time of year.
The grass is green and the smell is sweet.
Out comes the lawn mower to keep it neat.
In the summer the weather is hot
And we can go swimming quite a lot.
We can build sandcastles and swim in the sea
And then buy an ice cream just for me.
Now it's Autumn and the leaves are brown
And the squirrels are collecting nuts on the ground.
In winter the Christmas tree is covered in tinsel for all to see.
Then the snow comes down and everything is white
And Santa Claus will come tonight.

Katie Morton (7)
Ashford CE Primary School

FOOTBALL

Football is my favourite game,
Me and my friends feel the fame.
We go to the green to play ball,
and we put the goal next to the wall.
Even though I have to run,
it is lots of fun.
Sometimes I let my brother play,
his name is Jack,
But I always put him at the back.
My friend Ben, thinks he's the best,
but I know I'm better than the rest.

George Barratt (7)
Ashford CE Primary School

RAINBOW POEM

Red is the colour of the reddest red rose,
As red as a ruby ring.

Orange is as juicy as a peach,
As nice as an orange drink.

Yellow is the colour of the blazing, hot sun,
As good as a lemon ice lolly.

Green is the freshest cress,
With all the lovely taste.

Blue is the sky,
Where you see the planes go by.

Indigo is a nice spring flower
Swaying in the cold, cold mist.

Violet is a beautiful sunset,
Rising in the sky.

Lauren Thomas (8)
Ashford CE Primary School

MEGAN'S DOLPHIN POEM

Dolphins go up and down,
Dolphins can swim around,
Dolphins can hop and sing,
Dolphins can do anything.

I wish I had one for a pet,
But I would have to have a pond, I bet.
To have such a big animal, I think, would be very cool,
But Mum says it would be a bit of a handful.

Megan Horsley (7)
Ashford CE Primary School

THE WEATHER WAR

Spring, spring - when the sun is king.
He sits on his throne,
And whines and moans he got rid of the rain,
Oh what a shame.

The flowers will die,
On the ground they will lie.
The sun goes mad
He asks the rain to help
And the rain is glad.

The rain comes through,
The sun helps too.
The flowers grow back,
They're on the right track.
Now the sun and rain are friends once again.

Joe Gannon (8)
Ashford CE Primary School

RAINBOW POEM

Red is a red Valentine rose, silky and light.
Orange is a smooth orange as round as a clock.
Yellow is a hot blazing sun, shining upon us.
Green is green swaying grass, blowing in the wind.
Blue is a deep ocean crashing on the shore where children play.
Indigo is a butterfly fluttering through the trees,
Eating and drinking.
Violet is a flower which glimmers in the sun, happily swaying.

George Jennings (8)
Ashford CE Primary School

RAINBOW POEM

Red is as red as a rose,
Nice and silky and soft.

Orange is an orange, juicy as fruit.

Yellow is as bright as the sun,
Shining in my eyes.

Green is as green as grass,
And it grows.

Blue is as blue as sky,
And very bright.

Indigo is the colour of a butterfly,
Nice and shiny.

Violet is a purple colour, in the rainbow.

Alexandra Hills (8)
Ashford CE Primary School

RAINBOW POEM

Red is a loving Valentine heart,
With love from a man with the red jam tart.
Orange is the sun near the sea,
Maybe there will be a kiss for you and me.
Yellow is a daffodil swaying left and right,
You didn't give money, try not to be tight.
Green is the fresh dew on the grass,
You go away to the grass but forget your swimming pass.
Blue is the ocean, that doesn't give out a lotion.
Indigo is blue with purple, it could be the colour of a whirlpool.
Violet is purple all alone, and you're out of this poem's tone.

Max Hill (9)
Ashford CE Primary School

RAINBOW POEM

Red is a beautiful Valentine heart like some roses.
Orange is like the sand at the sunny beach,
Blowing in people's eyes.
Yellow is as bright as the sun,
Blazing under the clouds.
Green is the colour of the wet soggy grass
Next to the mud.
Blue is as blue as a kingfisher fluttering
In the windy sky.
Indigo is a butterfly,
Flying under a big, big tree.
Violet is the colour of a woodland flower
Blowing in the breeze.

George Owen (8)
Ashford CE Primary School

RAINBOW POEM

Red is as red as a shiny red apple
Hard and strong.
Orange is a juicy tangerine,
Round and soft.
Yellow is as bright as the sunset.
Green is the new grass.
Blue is the light sky,
Cloudy as could be.
Indigo is as nice as a butterfly
In the grey sky.
Violet is the colour of grapes and very juicy.

Paige Chipping (9)
Ashford CE Primary School

RAINBOW POEM

Red is a soft rose,
With sharp spiky edges.

Orange is a setting sun,
With all the people eating their tea.

Yellow is the beach,
Where the dogs swim in the sea.

Green is the grass,
With all the bugs in it.

Blue is the sparkling sea
With all the fish in it.

Indigo is a flower in a big field.

Violet is grapes, with big pips inside.

John Lane (9)
Ashford CE Primary School

RAINBOW POEM

Red is as red as a bright red rose
Orange is like sand on the beach
Blowing in everybody's eyes.
Yellow is like bright paint
Running down the paper.
Green is as green as blazing grass
Blowing everywhere.
Blue is as blue as deep raspberries,
Being picked by everybody.
Indigo is a bright flower in the grass.
Violet is a nice butterfly flying in the air.

Hannah Bliss (8)
Ashford CE Primary School

RAINBOW POEM

Red is the colour of a blazing sunset,
Glistening in the water.

Orange is the colour of the ripest tangerine,
Good enough to eat.

Yellow is the colour of the sun,
Beaming in the midday sky.

Green is the colour of the freshest grass,
Dancing in the wind.

Blue is the colour of the coolest crystal water,
Straight from the rivers.

Indigo is the colour of a fluttering butterfly,
Floating in the breeze.

Violet is the colour of a woodland flower
Bouncing in the wind.

Morgan Price-King (9)
Ashford CE Primary School

RAINBOW POEM

Red is a lovely juicy ripe apple
Orange is sour and juicy
Yellow is the blazing sun shining
On the beautiful yellow cornfield.
Green is the swaying grass.
Blue as the bluest sky in the world.
Indigo is the colour of the best flowers.
Violet is the colour of a butterfly flying over.

Hannah Soan (9)
Ashford CE Primary School

RAINBOW POEMS

R is for red, as soft as the red rose
In the sun under the tree.

O is for orange, juicy and squidgy,
And tastes lovely when you eat it.

Y is for yellow, as bright sparkling sun
Shining on everything it sees.

G is for green, as wet soggy grass
When it is raining, lovely to eat for the animals.

B is for blue, as the transparent deep blue sea.

I is for indigo, a flower just like it has been born.

V is for violet, the colour of some grapes
Tasty enough to eat.

Matthew Jones (8)
Ashford CE Primary School

RAINBOW POEM

Red is a red Valentine rose,
Red is a dragon's red-hot fire.
Orange is a juicy fruit all round and soft inside
And hard on the outside.
Yellow is the blazing hot sun shining on the flowers.
Green is the grass, with frogs on it croaking.
Blue is the water, cool and clear.
Blue is the sky where the clouds go by.
Indigo is a flower and a butterfly looking for pollen.
Violet is the grape, fresh from vines.

Jordan Bishop (8)
Ashford CE Primary School

RAINBOW POEM

Red is as red as a Valentine heart
Shiny and soft.

Orange is a juicy tangerine
Completely nutritious.

Yellow is the blazing sun,
Shining brightly.

Green is a sniffy meadow
Wavy all day.

Blue is the salty ocean
Cold and wavy.

Indigo is like my bedroom
Cold and hard.

Violet is my favourite plant
Muddy and weary.

Kelly Srnecz (9)
Ashford CE Primary School

RAINBOW POEM

Red is a juicy apple, full of taste and juice.
Orange is the hot sun, blazing through summer.
Yellow is a luscious lemon, which you can squeeze
                                    into lemon juice.
Green is fresh grass, swaying through the breeze.
Blue is the great deep ocean, crashing onto the shore.
Indigo is a beautiful butterfly fluttering through the cold breeze.
Violet is the flowers of spring, standing proud in the ground.

Robert Anderson (9)
Ashford CE Primary School

Rainbow Poem

Red is the Valentine's rose,
Silky and soft.
Orange is the orange tangerine,
Sweet and round as a disco ball.
Yellow is the yellowest sun,
In the midday sky.
Green is the darkest grass,
Blazing in the spring meadow.
Blue is the bluest fresh water,
From the lake underneath the blue sky.
Indigo is the most beautiful butterfly
On a plant on the ground underneath a summer tree.
Violet is a plant upon the ground, in the blazing sun.

Nicholas Jones (8)
Ashford CE Primary School

Through The Woods

I was walking home on Hallowe'en night through the woods,
When suddenly I got a fright through the woods.
I started to run through the woods.
My body turned numb through the woods,
Vines with thorns grew through the woods.
I heard crashing horns through the woods.
I felt bones through the woods,
There were groans through the woods.
Arrgh!
Something had got me through the woods,
I was struggling for life through the woods,
I felt the blade of a knife through the woods,
I fell back through the woods,
It had turned black through the woods.

Eliot Hill (10)
Bush Hill Park Primary School

COME ALL YE PARLIAMENT

In the year 2002
Will life be the same?
Peter M and the passport,
For his job he really fought.
Tony B and the tomato
Splattered on his back,
I bet the woman who threw it,
Had lots in her sack.
Will Ken L win his match?
Will the pigeons make a fight?
I bet it will be a disgusting sight.
Gordon B is the man with the loot
Gordon's handout will buy my dad a new suit.
William told us about his fourteen beers
I hope it won't harm his career.
Only time will really tell
And until the last bell
All politicians will lose their appeal.

Stephen King (11)
Bush Hill Park Primary School

WHAT IS PURPLE?

Purple is a fat juicy plum that squirts out on your teeth.
Purple is a fat tropical fish that waves its tail in sea everywhere.
Purple is fireworks that fire in the Millennium sky.
Purple is silk and velvet that rules softly against your smooth skin.
Purple is the purple heart that is honoured with bravery.
Purple is coldness that goes right through your stomach.
Purple is a feeling that glows on everyone.
Purple is for violet, that grows tall in the grass.

Avani Jariwala (10)
Bush Hill Park Primary School

DEVIL, ANGEL AND BOY

Listen boy,
Steal money from your Mum's purse.
Eat with your fingers
Burp and make other rude noises,
And for the last thing,
Only listen to what I say!
Said Devil to boy.

Listen young boy,
Help the poor and the old,
Do useful things around the house,
Always say thank you and please.
But listen to me,
Never listen to what the Devil has to say!
Said Angel to boy.

Why are you both here?
I only came to post some letters,
Said boy to Devil and Angel.

And off ran the boy, home.

Clare Daly (11)
Bush Hill Park Primary School

COLLECTION

On the meadows lay the sailors, bones,
While the dead cry help me moans.
The sirens wait for another victim by the cliffs
So this story adds to the collection of myths.

Natasha Robinson (10)
Bush Hill Park Primary School

TREPEAZATHAN

A big blue monster with red spots
And a long green mane with lots of knots.
It has long claws
And often gnaws,
On dogs bones
And small cats.
He has ten spikes upon its back,
That feels just like a blazing rack.
He has a long tail,
With a huge nail,
Sticking out the end.
His one big eye
Covered in yellow dye,
Is always open wide.
There is no more to tell,
But he has an awful yell.
As the night draws in
He sleeps for his last time.

Elizabeth Beggs (10)
Bush Hill Park Primary School

HERE'S AND THERE'S

Here's a table - there's a chair,
There's a rabbit - here's a hare.
There's my blanket and there's my bed.
Now I'm going to rest my head.
                    Goodnight!

Vincenza De Falco (10)
Bush Hill Park Primary School

WHEN COLOUR FADES TO GREY

When highlights stand out of the front of the page
When sirens go far out the land
When faces turn grey and the tears run down
When colour fades to grey
When colour fades to grey.

When planes come whizzing around the corner
And drop bombs on our little house
When rain and wind strongly appear
When colour fades to grey,
When colour fades to grey.

When schoolchildren hide under their school desks
And wait for the sirens to stop
The children get scared as the sirens go on
When colour fades to grey
When colour fades to grey.

Rhonda-Topaz Davis (9)
Bush Hill Park Primary School

WHO HAS SEEN A CAKE TALK?

Who has seen a cake talk?
Neither I nor you
But when the night is right
You hear them talk about
How they look and taste.

Who has seen a cake talk?
Neither I nor you
They talk so quiet just like a mouse
Talking to the cheese.
All you hear is chit-chat.

Cara Strickland (10)
Bush Hill Park Primary School

THE FIRST MEN ON MARS

Y - we come in peace from the four planet.
Take us to your leader now!

Y - it's very hot! Yes it is hot.

Y - Look a rubber model of a solar beam with
colourful light.

- Horror Horror.

Y - where we come from it is blue, green and white
You see the blue is 'sea' green is 'land,'
White is 'clouds' over the sea and the land.

Y - look at men.

Y - we come in peace from the four planet.

Y - I am the alien of this planet.
See my head I have two so I can see better.

Y - so now go or we will chop off your head with our sharp teeth.

Jack Ridler (11)
Bush Hill Park Primary School

ROBOT IN A TREE

A tourist came in from Mars,
It parked in a tree, and said:

'The creatures of this star
are made of feathers.

Through all the feathers
you can see their skin.

Their feathers are brown and move on wings.

Big beaks, dark with a hole.

They have two eyes
White marbles with black dots.

I've had enough with this planet
It's too small.'

Mathew Elsey Hood (11)
Bush Hill Park Primary School

FLUFFY THE PUPPY

Fluffy is a puppy, full of love and joy
He bounces like a rubber ball
And never hears me when I call
Sit! Stay! Fetch!
But always hears me when
I say 'Good boy have a biscuit'
And when the day is over,
He snuggles on my lap.
So I wrap him in his blanket
All snug and quietly sleeping.

Sophie Lawrence (10)
Bush Hill Park Primary School

SHARK

If you ever walk along a beach,
And run into a shark.
You had better keep your mouth shut
And don't let your dog bark.
Just step away quietly,
Step away from it.
You don't want to be the new one
The next one that it bit.
So don't ever walk along a beach
Alone and in the hump
'Cause if you run into a shark
He will only say
        Chomp!

Robert Fairweather (11)
Bush Hill Park Primary School

HOW TO BE A POLITE PERSON

Please be polite;
Just give a little bite.
Pick it with a fork,
Wipe the juice that may trickle down your
chubby chin.
It is ready and ripe.
Whenever you are.
You will need a knife and fork
And spool and plate or napkin
and tablecloth.
So just eat! eat! eat!
But be polite!

Saziye Ergider (10)
Bush Hill Park Primary School

HOW TO SLURP SOUP

Sit up straight, lift up your chin
Get ready to bite right in
The first thing you need to know
Is that soup should slowly flow
Right down your throat and to your tum
Where all your other food should come.

Lift your bowl up to your lips
Your stomach should be doing flips.
The excitement would transform a nun
Into a little monster full of fun!
Hurrah you think, it's mine at last
(It should disappear extremely fast)

You slurp, you bury, you writhe and wriggle.
This drama starts to make you giggle!
Your tummy expands into a ball
The weight begins to make you fall!
You slowly gain a ton
Your face turns yellow as the sun!

Alice Perry (11)
Bush Hill Park Primary School

SUNNY DAYS

I love sunny days
Hot sun, blue skies
That reveal a hot air
I love sunny days
Day trips out and about
Long paddles in small paddling pools,
And ice rockets that take off in your mouth.
Yes I love sunny days.

Abby Feben (10)
Bush Hill Park Primary School

A WITCH'S SPELL

Double, double, toil and trouble,
Fire burn and cauldron bubble.
A frog's leg slimy and green,
Lions cooked but still quite mean.
Eye of fish and tail of cat
Half a dog and one big rat.
Smelly slugs and a wasp's great sting,
Dirty snails and a bird's great wing.
To stir a charm of harmful trouble,
Like a death spell boil and bubble.
Double, double, toil and trouble,
Fire burn and cauldron bubble.

Chloe Wood (11)
Bush Hill Park Primary School

WHAT IS BLUE?

This is blue
Blue is the sea
Surfer's wild
Blue is the sky
Clear as the eye
Blue is the flower
Swaying in the wind
Blue is the ink
On the writer's wrist
Blue are the tears
Splashing down my cheeks.
That is blue.

Cem Ibrahim (10)
Bush Hill Park Primary School

AUGUST POEM

Today it is raining
and it is autumn.
The children are going back to school
with their new bags and their new uniforms.
It is spring for the children and autumn for the teachers.
For the children are always young and the teachers
                                    are growing older.
And the blackboard is grazing with chalk.
The teachers look out at the rainy playground
and sometimes they think about Macbeth,
but mostly about their own lives,
and how the freshness of spring has departed.
It is raining
and it is autumn
and the rain prickles the sea
and wets the new uniforms of the children
and their new shoes.
When it is raining the soul becomes grey,
a continuous drizzle of autumn.
It is like a screen that will always be there.
The teachers look out the forgotten chalk in their hands
                        and they break it over and over.

Sajel Bhatti (8)
Coston Primary School

MIDNIGHT

In space the darkness is pitch-black
Like a deep, black hole in the middle of the earth,
Like a muddy claw coming towards you
Like a frightening shadow below the moonlight
Like a beam of lightning in the sky.

Holly Young (9)
Coston Primary School

ODE TO A TEDDY

Oh to a teddy how silky you feel
I could never touch any other like you,
Even if I see one I can never ever buy it,
And if I do I'll always deny it.
Oh teddy, oh teddy you're so cuddly
How I adore you you're so soft
Oh teddy I love you
No one can take you
Oh teddy, oh teddy I love you so
You are so smart you really are
You smell so sweet
And with your lovely velvet burgundy bow
You're like an angel fluttering low.
I cannot sleep without you.
I take you everywhere I do, I do
Oh my teddy I love you so.

Katie Susanne Treadwell (10)
Coston Primary School

DARKNESS

In space, the darkness is pitch-black
Like a black paper bin filled up with rubbish.
The sky coloured charcoal, like the bushes in Africa,
Like a spooky, frightening nightmare.
Like many chairs coloured black and laid in a hole.
But that's how darkness is scary.

Maya Kulemeka (10)
Coston Primary School

HOMEWORK

Homework! Homework! I hate homework!
Homework is boring,
It makes me feel like snoring.
I get homework every day,
Monday, Tuesday, Wednesday, Thursday, Friday.
Homework takes so long I'd like to creep,
To have a snack when everyone's asleep.
I feel like looking out of my window
And then find myself squashing my pillow.
Homework is so boring I think I'll do all that,
And of course it is better than finding a rat.

Laveen Khailany (10)
Coston Primary School

SURPRISED

One little horsey galloping in the field.
Two bees flying in the sky.
Three colours lighting the sky.
Four tea cups on the table.
Five pennies in the purse.
Six people eating honey.
Seven bats finding their vampires.
Eight leaves falling on the ground.
Nine flowers in the shops.
Ten men in a farm
And that is it.

Serene El-Kurd (9)
Coston Primary School

An Ode To My Soft Toy

Oh my soft cuddly toy you guard me with such might
You guard me in the night.
You keep me warm when I'm cold.
You're soft, so you're not hard to hold.
I play with you in the daytime when I'm bored.
I treat you and play with you like a lord.
You play games with me that no one likes.
You never hurt me, you're as quiet as a kite.
You never get grumpy in the day.
You never get in my way.
I desire your smooth shiny yellow coat.
I take you everywhere even on a ferry boat.
I adore the way you smile even when I'm cross
You think whenever I am I'm the boss.
Your hard crispy tail, your soft toes, your sparkling eyes.
You stay put wherever you are even if you don't want to.
Oh my soft cuddly toy.

Sumeiyeh Al-Zobaiydi (10)
Coston Primary School

Colours, Colours

Colours are good to see them
Colours make you feel happy
Colours make you feel sad
Colours are for happiness
Colours are there for sadness
But colours are there forever
So love colours and you will love life
Because it's with us for ever.

Sejal Hirani (8)
Coston Primary School

BEDTIME

Bedtime is the time for peace.
Bedtime is the time to shut your eyes,
and go to sleep.
You keep your eyes shut really tight
and sleep until morning light.
'Mum' I called 'I can't sleep!'
'Just close your eyes and try counting sheep!'
I like to dream of something nice,
Like riding on a motorbike.
The windows were open, my curtains were blowing,
I ducked under my covers, there was something moving.
But it was only the shadows on the wall,
That nearly made me lose my cool.
And now I close my eyes to sleep
And start again to count the sheep.

Amy McGinness (8)
Coston Primary School

NIGHT

In space the darkness is pitch-black.
Like a spit dribbling greyhound.
Like a charcoal black night rider burning rubber.
Like a speedy, rapid rat running through the forest midnight.
Like an unknown predator hunting for its dead food.
In space the darkness is pitch-black.

Ricky Banbury (9)
Coston Primary School

THE NIGHT SKY

The night sky is ebony black
Like a gorilla's hairy back.
Dark and scary like an orange fierce lion.
All the silver stars glistening and sparkling
in the night sky.
In the night sky the moon brightens your face.
In the night sky people dance
and have parties with joy in the moonlight.
In the night sky the moon smiles at you like an old
crooked lady and she says
    'Goodnight'

Raveen Khailany (9)
Coston Primary School

MIDNIGHT

In space the darkness is pitch-black
Like a sky scraper
Like a gigantic hand moving his shadow
Right over the whole entire universe.
Like a midnight rat covered in charcoal
Who will never stand out in midnight,
And like a shiny, silver, crimson, grey
Wolf howling as midnight comes.
In space the darkness is pitch-black
Always.

Azeem Bhati (10)
Coston Primary School

MIDNIGHT DARKNESS

In space the darkness is pitch-black
like the sky with no shining silver moon
and no glittering star.
Like a black hole floating in space
Like a piece of black charcoal
Like a black shadow following you.

Sheena Hanley (9)
Coston Primary School

NIGHT

In space the darkness is pitch-black
Like a dusky black sky without any stars
Like a dark house without lights
Like a glistening navy car without any headlights
Like a dark spooky cave
In space the darkness is pitch-black.

Sarika Khanna (9)
Coston Primary School

NIGHT

In space the darkness is pitch-black
Like aliens invading to blow up the world.
Like a big black shadow coming to haunt you down.
Like an owl making scary noises.
Like a person having a bad nightmare.

Aaron Thomas J Esprit (9)
Coston Primary School

THE NIGHT

In space the darkness is pitch-black
(Like charcoal pitch-black man eating sharks)
in the glittering, slivery, shining stars.
Like a frightening lion catching its prey.
Like a person having a nightmare.
Like a owl howling in pain.
In space the darkness is pitch-black.

Mohammed Mian (10)
Coston Primary School

MIDNIGHT

In space the darkness is pitch-black
Like a black ink pot
Like space without any twinkling silver stars
Like an old, tattered, frightening, spooky, haunted house.
Like a bump in the night
In space the darkness is pitch-black.

Huda Taher (9)
Coston Primary School

MIDNIGHT

In space the darkness is pitch-black
Like a big shadow coming to haunt you down
Like a nightmare coming to kill you
Like a haunting ghost in the graveyard
Like a scary dark night.

Darrly Payas (10)
Coston Primary School

AN ODE TO MY PENCIL CASE

Oh my smooth pencil case!
How silky you are on my fingertips.
How sweet and divine you smell,
How flexible you are.
Your beautiful blue sparkly colour,
With a lighter blue on the ends
Of your slim cylinder figure.
Your gorgeous Angel sign in silver.
Your zip puller that always catches my eye.
How warm you embrace my pencils.
The slight move they make when you open.
Oh how I love this, wonderful pencil case.
My pencil case.

Stevie Strutton (10)
Coston Primary School

NIGHT

In space the darkness is pitch-black

Like an azure sky turning to a navy monster
turning to a charcoal-black killer whale.

Like a big black hole sucking the glittering silver stars
and the icy silver moon
Like a screaming black eagle.

Like a black, fire-breathing dragon
devouring his meal in space
the darkness is pitch-black.

Jorel Paul (10)
Coston Primary School

An Ode To My Life

Life is a gift - respect it.
Life is a game - play it.
Life is a song - sing it.
Life is a picture - draw it.
Life is a puzzle - solve it.
Life is a bell - ring it.
Life is a treasure - keep it.
Life is a seed - grow it.
Life is a garden - look after it.
Life is a lesson - learn it.
Life is good - use it.

Sepand Bastani (10)
Coston Primary School

Ode To A TV

Oh to the colour TV where would we be without you?
Your boring history channels
Your sizzling cooking stations.
Documentary and soaps leave me in a twist.
But on sky digital I get all the loving help I need.
Let's just hope you don't leave us, me and my brother plead.
I will never be apart from you,
For the rest of the time I live.
Let's just hope that's a long time my darling TV.
My TV.

Luke Pepper (11)
Coston Primary School

AN ODE TO MY TEDDY

Oh my furry little friend!
How blue you are.
Your big long ears and your little mouth.
I like when you hop around with your little feet.
When I cuddle you my little rabbit
I feel lots of love from you.
You're so soft and cuddly.
You're simply my favourite.
You guard me in the night
My little friend.

Oh my soft cuddly rabbit.

James Armstrong (11)
Coston Primary School

AN ODE TO MY HAT

Oh precious hat I adore you so
I promise I will never let you go!
It took a second to notice you in the shop
It took a minute to like you
Oh how I adore you.
But it would take a whole lifetime to forget you!
I like the way you keep my head warm.
I like the way you mess up my hair.
Your beautiful red sparkling Nike tick.
The way you stretch when I put you on my head.
Oh I adore you dear hat.

Luke O'Brien (10)
Coston Primary School

An Ode To My Shoes

My wonderful, wonderful tap shoes
They are on my special menu.
Like fish and chips and lovely cookies,
And my divine ice cream.
Sometimes I take my tap shoes and
I sing 'Halabaloo, halabaloo'
My tap shoes with their lovely tapping rhythm.
They sparkle like lovely treasured stars
Shine like the gloomy sun.
My lovely glittery, sparkly golden tap shoes.
Sometimes I sleep in the night and hold it tight.
My divine, divine tap shoes.

Linda Opoku (10)
Coston Primary School

Ode To My Teddy Bear

Oh sweet bear,
How warm your black fur feels.
Silky hairs tickle my face.
Rosy red bow is red as a flame.
Black fur as black as the night.
Bear, oh sweet bear comforts me during the night.
Wind howling, storm blowing he cuddles me tight
                              to keep me calm
And eventually I fall asleep and he rolls on the floor.

Emily Marsh (10)
Coston Primary School

MY FAVOURITE ANIMALS

Dogs chase cats and cats run away.
I don't know where but far far away.
Chimpanzees climb all the trees
Monkeys do but they nick all the bananas off them.
Pigs are pink but cows are black and white,
but horses I must say,
they're full of the colour brown.

Stephanie Strobridge (8)
Coston Primary School

NIGHT

In space the darkness is pitch-black
Like a frightening shadow underneath the moon
Like a haunting ghost in the graveyard
Like a silver flash of lightning
Like a glittering gold star
In space the darkness is pitch-black.

Hamish Daniel (9)
Coston Primary School

MIDNIGHT

In space the darkness is pitch-black
Like a haunted house with no lights
Like a big deep hole that never ends
Like a glittering gold bangle but dirty
Like a howl from a wolf at the strike of midnight.
In space the darkness is pitch-black.

Jade Englezos (10)
Coston Primary School

ODE TO...

Oh computer you are the only thing
That matters to me.
Your smooth surface around the screen.
The things you type, you type one hundred and one things
that mean everything to me.
You have a dictionary with one thousand and two words.
Oh computer you have everything I need.

Sophie Henson (10)
Coston Primary School

MIDNIGHT

In the space the darkness is pitch-black
Like a haunting ghost in your pitch-black house.
Like a wrinkly hand coming to get you.
Like a flood coming up your face.
Like a knife floating in the air.
In the space the darkness is pitch-black.

Rachel Davies (9)
Coston Primary School

DARKNESS

In space the darkness is pitch black,
Like a big jumper full of black cotton,
Like a big glittering gold star,
Like a person having a nightmare,
Like a haunted house!
In space the darkness is pitch-black.

Alexander Azadbakht (10)
Coston Primary School

OH MY LOVELY TELEVISION

Oh my lovely television
You are so bright
When I touch the control
I'll be there all night.
You amuse me with EastEnders, Popstars,
Big Brother, Brookside, music channels,
Shipwrecked, Sister Sister, Kenan and Kel.
Moesha and Ali G.
The bright colours catch my eye,
And I feel like floating in the misty sky.
You also beguile me with it being 32 inches
And widescreen with the wonderful pictures.
Oh my lovely television I'm glad you're mine.

Natalie Bolam (11)
Coston Primary School

MY BED

Oh my wonderful bed.
I cannot live without you.
You make me feel safe
When I'm sleeping at night.
When I set eyes on you
I knew you were the one for me.
Your covers are fluffy and warm
Your mattress as bouncy as a bouncy ball.
My wonderful bed.

James Brown (10)
Coston Primary School

THE SEA

The misty cold sea
Hitting against the rock,
People laying in the sunlight
As the sea laps at their feet
But as the sun drops deep into the sea
A white hunting moon appears to shine upon
the darkest black of the sea.
Underneath deep down below,
Where none of us will go
The fish swim to and fro
They are happy and soft within the sea
So although we fear the sea,
The fish think it heavenly.

Chelsea Cox (9)
Coston Primary School

OH TEETH

Oh teeth.

How lovely you can be
I'm sorry I'll never eat chocolate again or . . .
I didn't mean to make you rotten,
By now you could be clean and sparkly.
I didn't want it to be this way.
I'm going to have a filling
From then on you'll be the only one in my life.
I'll eat five fruits a day
Just so we can be friends again
Oh my teeth.

Victoria Whenman (10)
Coston Primary School

STARS

Stars are bright they light up your sight.
When the street is dark
it lights up the whole park.
You need to switch off your light
so the stars can be bright.
Starts are flashing and if you look
they are so smashing.
Stars, stars can travel to Mars
but they will always come back.

Nitya Manani (9)
Coston Primary School

MY DAD IS TV MAD!

My dad is TV mad,
But he says it is bad
My brother and I don't take any notice of him,
Because what he knows is very slim!
Every night when I go to bed
I hear my dad laughing off his head.
No wonder I never get any sleep,
He is lucky I don't make a peep.

Jessica Banfield (9)
Coston Primary School

JANUARY

J anuary is on my birthday
A nd May is my friend's birthday
N ovember is on my sister's birthday
U ncle's and Aunty's birthdays all the way round.
A pril is Easter time when we look forward to chocolate
and bunnies.
R ain is on December when you're sad and grumpy
Y ellow is the sunshine that comes in August.

Nenna Tateri (9)
Coston Primary School

FRUITS

Apple, apple, so red and rosy.
Orange, orange, so juicy and sweet.
Banana, banana so yellow and squishy.
Grapes, grapes so squashy and purple.
Mango, mango so orange and bright.
Peas, peas, so green and hard.
Do you like fruits because they are healthy?

Homa Bastani (8)
Coston Primary School

KIDS!

Kids, kids, glorious kids,
Some people love them
Some people hate them
Depends if you're either
Miss Honey or
Miss Trunchball.
If you're a kid you'll know
What I'm talking about.

Myself I love kids,
Well I don't love them,
but I like them
That's because I am one
Kids,
Kids,
Glorious
Kids.

Jade Bonnett (11)
Echelford Primary School

THE FROG

I am a frog
I am as green as a leaf
I like the water
because it is as cool as ice.

A tree is like a big monster to me
It is green and brown like green grass and mud.

I do not like being small
because people could not see me in the bushes,
They can step on me.

Kirsty Newman (8)
Echelford Primary School

POLLUTION

What flows in our rivers is pollution.
So I came up with a solution.
If you see a tin,
throw it in the nearest bin.
All the horrible pollution which flows
in our river
Is affecting our river's liver.
All our rivers flow like dribbles.
Soon all we will have left is nibbles.
All our juicy fruits,
With no water, they will have no roots.
All our animals are going to die.
So let our rivers flow high.
I hope you people reply.

Jack Lawrance
Echelford Primary School

DOLPHINS

D olphins swim in a graceful way,
O n the ocean waves they play,
L eaping, diving with their friends,
P erfect animals till the end.
H appy to be free in the sea,
I ntelligent creatures like you and me,
N ature is their middle name,
S o I hope you don't play the hunting game.

Charlotte McCormack (10)
Echelford Primary School

WINTER

One winter cold morning,
Ice and snow was dawning,
There were no colours outside,
All was just bare.
It seemed that all of the flowers were so rare.

There were lots of icicles so tiny,
But glistened oh so shiny,
All outside there was a blanket of frost,
The only colour peeping out was slippery green moss.

There were no animals,
They'd all fallen asleep.
The hedgehogs had all run,
The foxes were all hidden.
And only a few animals ventured inside.
People were cold and huddled to get warm by their fire,
Longing for summer,
That is their desire.

In winter you can go places,
Do things like skating on ice or having snowball fights.
Sliding down hills and crashing in snow,
There must be warmer places to go.

Winter is a happy time when Santa is on his way,
He brings all gifts big and small,
And that's the part I love most of all.

Lewis Shaw (10)
Echelford Primary School

MY NEW SCHOOL

When I moved to Ashford, I felt alone and sad,
I then went to Echelford, and started feeling glad.
Mr Wilson smiled at me, then he showed us round,
I looked up at Mum and Dad but didn't make a sound.

I then saw all the children and spotted Jess and Louise
They looked so very friendly, and soon put me at ease.
They've both been very kind to me and I've even been for tea,
I've played in both their bedrooms and met their families.

I've made so many good friends, although they are my best,
And hope when we all change new schools,
We'll keep in touch and do our best.

Although I liked my last school and sometimes I was bored,
I'm really glad I started here at the wonderful . . .
. . . Echelford.

Lauren Brown (11)
Echelford Primary School

CHOCOLATE

I like chocolate it's nice for a treat,
Especially from the corner shop just down the street
White chocolate, milk chocolate, plain chocolate bars,
I would like anything, even a Mars!

Swirling, twirling hot milk chocolate,
Lick it off the spoon and feel the sensation,
Melting in the mouth, it tastes divine,
Couldn't be better. What a creation!

Edward Ackers (11)
Echelford Primary School

WHAT DO I WANT TO BE

It was making a cup of tea
When I realised what I wanted to be.

I want to be a footballer
all the glamour and fame
It's people like *David Beckham*
Who cares just for money
not about the true colours of the game.

I want to be policeman
with all the cuffs and pepper spray.
Think about the respect I'll get day by day.

Or maybe I'll be a scientist
dealing with hydrochloric acid
Maybe I'll become a film star
starring in films like Lake Placid.

No I'll be a pop star and be No 1

My goal at the moment is to have fun.
I don't know what I'll be
I guess I just have to wait and see!

Stuart Osborne (11)
Echelford Primary School

MY BEDROOM

My bedroom is my favourite place,
In there I rest my head.
Every morning when I wake up,
I like to read in bed.

I've got teddies all upon my bed,
My toys are on the floor.
My books are on the bookshelves,
And posters on the door.

My bedroom's blue and yellow,
I think it's really cool.
I like to chill out in my room,
When I come home from school.

Kathryn Ringshaw (10)
Echelford Primary School

THE MATCH

We're off to the football match,
The train is very slow,
But in the end we get there,
With half an hour to go.

The kick-off has been taken,
I hope that Arsenal win.
'Cos if they don't I will have to
Throw my programme in the bin.

Here comes Bould down the wing,
He crosses into the box.
Bergkamp running to the ball,
Like a raging ox.

We score, Yippee! Yippee!
Now it's half-time.
Nothing happened in the second half
And the game finished at half-past nine.

Ben Skipper (11)
Echelford Primary School

HOMES

When you roam around a house,
You probably won't even see a mouse.
Somewhere, you may see a football
And somewhere else you may even see a tennis ball.
If you waddle off to another room,
You may even see some perfume.
In there you might see a stereo,
And if you walk along you could see a radio.
In that room you could see a bed,
And it is a very nice place to rest your head.
When you go to another room, you could see a light,
But be careful because if it's a 100 watts, it would be bright.
Close to a TV you could see a satellite
And watching it will be a delight.

Graham Neville (10)
Echelford Primary School

THE DRAGON

A dragon is like an enormous volcano ready to spurt and explode,
Jagged, sharp, razor-like spikes on his crumbly, scaly, dark green back,
As its earthquaking roar tremors through the world and galaxy,
Its fiery dark yellowy-red breath burns the strongest, the biggest,
bit of metal (in a second) to a crisp.
Inside its stinking humongous stomach lie dead bodies
and dogs and cats, owners had lost months ago,
Its eyes with a devilish look in them
scanning for someone to catch and devour.
Its big, red, wide blood dripping mouth yawns
displaying bits of bone stuck in its razor-sharp teeth.

Joshua McNally-Rendle (11)
Echelford Primary School

FIREWORKS

Up high amongst the sky,
Come see the fireworks go by.
Big ones, small ones, you see them all
The crowd cheer, wow and cool!

The colours of the rainbow glowing in the sky
The colours of the rainbow up high,
Oh so high
Blue ones, orange ones, red ones, bang!

Still at the end, the biggest to come
The last one up amongst the sky
Roaring high, see it fly
Boom! Boom! Boom!
Red, purple, orange, blue, yellow, everywhere.
Up high amongst the sky.

Navdeep Kalsi (11)
Echelford Primary School

THE WORLD OUTSIDE

It's a hullabaloo outside I'm trying to watch TV
But I can't because of the wind
The wind is making the trees push each other over
It's chatting up the letterbox
It's making the rain push against the window and
It's making drumming noises.
It goes ping, bong, clang
I can't hear the TV
I wish the storm could stop!

Sarah Jenkins (10)
Echelford Primary School

OASIS

Through the sandy, hot desert I walk,
I hear sounds that make me cry with happiness.
The rustling trees, trickling water,
It becomes louder as I approach.

There it is the lush green trees spreading afar,
The sound and the smell of fruits lure me in.
I see the water it's clear as crystal,
This is my dream I've been waiting for.

I strip into barely nothing,
I hesitate, then I jump.
But instead of jumping into water I jump into the sand,
My dream is now over, was it a true dream?

Aaron Shutt (10)
Echelford Primary School

THE SPIDER

A spider is a very good hider
He loves roast insect, he hates toast.
We try to capture flies but when
We get to the drawer, flies get in the way.
Flies are like yummy eyes.
We spiders are like race cars.
Humans are wicked species.
They rescue our yummy teas,
The fly appears immaculately
and walks dilly-dally.
So please let us be, otherwise you'll be our tea
Even though we're spiders and we're very good hiders,
We are not frightened of you.

Nicholas Chambers (9)
Echelford Primary School

ANNE BOLEYN

She married a king,
And had lots of rings,
She also loved to dance and sing.

She wanted to be a singer,
But she grew an extra finger.

People said she was a witch,
She wanted to run away,
But she fell down a ditch.

Her husband found her,
And tried to drown her.
But that didn't work,
Then he had an idea,
To chop off her head,
He did.
Then . . . she was *dead!*

Jessica Boyes-Korkis (11)
Echelford Primary School

MY NAN!

My nan loves to dance and sing,
She has brown curly hair,
And lots of frilly skirts to wear.
My nan loves colourful flowers,
And reads the paper in her spare hours.
She has two brothers, two sisters.
And on her feet she has blisters.
My nan has nice new slippers,
And for her husband she cooks kippers.
She's not that bad really.

Mercedes Cobbing (10)
Echelford Primary School

MY BEST FRIEND

My sister was born on the 12th of May,
She was born quite small but now she's okay.
She's learning to crawl,
She's nearly there.
Soon she'll learn to climb the stairs.
Her little world was just her mat,
So colourful and flat.
But now she's found the carpet.
It's blue and soft; a different touch,
She likes the feel so very much.

She'll soon be one,
That'll be fun.
She's into everything,
She's saying some words,
And likes to watch flying birds,
She's even cut two teeth.

She likes her food,
Which puts her in a good mood.
She dances, laughs and plays.
Her nickname is 'Squidia',
Her real name is Lydia,
She's a monkey in disguise.

She's always in trouble,
And likes to blow bubbles.
She's small and innocent,
She's a 'little pickle'.
She enjoys a little tickle,
She's always pulling faces,
She's sweet and kind to me,
'Cause she's my little 'Squidie',
And also she's my very best friend.

Jessica Dos Santos (10)
Echelford Primary School

ROSES ARE RED

Roses are red,
spiders are black,
don't look now,
there's one on your back.

Roses are red,
rats are brown,
we're on a cliff,
so don't look down.

Roses are red,
giraffes are tall,
if he sees you,
he'll spit on you all.

Roses are red,
mice are white,
we're on a mountain,
so they will have a fright.

Roses are red,
elephants are grey,
if he sees you,
he'll ask you to pay.

Roses are red,
whales are blue,
go for a swim,
then he'll like you.

Roses are red,
hippos are pink,
if he sees you,
he'll give you a wink.

Chris Woodford (11)
Echelford Primary School

MY BROTHER

My brother is a big pain,
He is a noisy chatterbox
And is always naughty.

He loves sausages
And he can't live without them.
I can't remember any dinner without sausages.

Sometimes he helps me clear up my bedroom,
But most of the time he watches my TV.

He watches TV all the time
He thinks about his tummy all the time
And he keeps asking questions.

I like my brother as he is
And I don't want him to change.
And he will always be my brother.

Tom Perman (11)
Echelford Primary School

A PUPPY

A puppy likes his food,
He eats it during the day,
If you don't take it out for walks
It gets in a mood,
In every way.

A puppy is very smart when it wants to be,
But when they come in from walks,
They're always muddy,
Forever and ever I will always love my puppy,
Even if it does come in all smelly.

Nicola Fogarty (10)
Echelford Primary School

THE RAINFOREST

My imagination lets me see trees
Slashing my sword all through the leaves.
A florist of sweetly scented flowers
Lovely tropical fruits, which taste for hours.
Chattering monkeys, squawking birds
Never saying a single word.
Trees which blow at the touch of the wind
The glazing sun in the air is pinned.
Bumpy bark, a cold steel sword
My rainforest dream at the end of the tour,
Goodbye dreamer, goodbye sword,
My rainforest friends are
Gone!

Stacey Mansell (10)
Echelford Primary School

DOUBLE BASS

A double bass is a funny old instrument
It has a long neck on an out of shape body.
Its curves are like a cat has been
practising it, scratching on it.
It has a big fat belly like a chubby sumo wrestler
When you bow it sounds like a dog barking.
But when you pluck it, it sounds more like
waves lapping against the sand.
Yes a double bass is a funny old instrument.

Mark O'Shea (10)
Echelford Primary School

CAT

I am a cat I'm really fat and my favourite food is fish.
I'll eat it every day, as well as birds.
Birds are fatty, nice and juicy.
Cats are as grey as storms,
Some are as black as night,
But us cats are all different.

But the adults are really big and horrid
But dogs are too.
Dogs are always chasing us
And mice are always annoying us,
Making me just want to eat them.
They might taste nice but they are sure hard to catch,
And really horrible looking.

Lisa Aspin (8)
Echelford Primary School

HARRY THE HAMSTER

Harry is cute and shaped as a furry ball
Harry is smooth and gentle
He sometimes bites if someone wakes him up
And grabs him, then he will bite you.

Harry the hamster is a mini monster
He tries to go under your armpit
But he is really nice
And everyone loves him.

My Harry!

Vineshree Amin (10)
Echelford Primary School

THE DUCK

The duck is like a swan and he is always having a little feast,
Also flapping its wings.
He eats bread as nice as a roll
Also likes little swims.

He tries to fly like a swan but he can't keep up.
He sleeps like a bird,
He's always awake like a fox.
He likes his friends.

He is very friendly like a butterfly.
He can move like a swan and paddle like a swan.

Zoe Lawrence (8)
Echelford Primary School

MONSTER

There's a monster in my bedroom, Mum
I'll tell you what it's like.
Its head is like a dragonfly
Its body is like a squirty worm.
Its claws are like a shark's tooth.
Its teeth are like red raw fire.
I know you don't believe me Mum
But hurry up, it's getting closer
It's aaarrrggghhh!

Leanne Coward (10)
Echelford Primary School

HUMPTY DUMPTY

Humpty Dumpty sat on a wall,
Humpty Dumpty had a great fall.
All the king's horses and all the king's men
Said 'Oh well, scrambled eggs for dinner again.'

In the pan went Mr Humpty
On the stove he sits
How long for nobody knows
But long enough to spit.

The men decided to have bacon
With their lovely meal.
So they started sizzling it,
And got a better deal.

Matthew Nesling (9)
Echelford Primary School

MY CHRISTMAS POEM

Christmas is a place where a jolly man flics across the sky.
Christmas time has a man flying in a ship.
Christmas has little Saint Nick gliding through the air.
Christmas is a time where Santa Claus is in his ship.
And Rudolf is his motor for it.
It anchors on houses,
So Santa can drop his presents in the stockings.

Ben Pearce (10)
Echelford Primary School

MY FAMILY

I'm watching TV
My brother's throwing paint at the wall,
Mum's down at the mall,
Dad's asleep,
And my little sister is singing Bo-Peep.

The dog's running downstairs,
A dustpan at his heels,
And some string around his neck.
Dad jumps out of bed and shouts 'What the heck!'

Mum comes home with a new comb,
Sees the paint on the wall, turns to me and says,
'Bad Boy Roy!'

James Pearce-Kelly (9)
Echelford Primary School

SPRING POEM

The flowers start to bloom,
So the bees will be here soon.
To suck out the pollen to take it to their hive,
Now everything comes alive.
The grass is dewy and green
What a beautiful picture to be seen!

Danielle Hill (9)
Echelford Primary School

A BUTTERFLY

A butterfly, a butterfly
Pretty like a sunset.
A mountain like an anthill
And a fox like a sharp toothed cat.

Some nectar like a sweet
That children like to eat
A twig like a tree
What is a home of a bee.

A butterfly, a butterfly
Like a colourful bird.
When it is as dark as night
It falls asleep in a flash.

Roxanne Carlin (8)
Echelford Primary School

THE SWAN

A swan is white as a cloud,
We eat fish all day.

We lay our eggs in the green,
We have long necks.
We have black eyes as black as night.
We have an orange beak.

We are not like any duck
Who wash their selves all day, or eat bread.

Jade Baylis (9)
Echelford Primary School

THE BEAUTIFUL RAINBOW

Red, orange, yellow, green
Keep it falling to your knee.
Blue, indigo and violet
A lovely little pirate.
Indigo is the sound of go!
Because it is indigo!
Red is a rose as hot as a nose.
Yellow is a buttercup and a pup.
And blue is true.
But what about orange?
And there's a rainbow.
That's a clue
Because that's orange too.

Florence Hunter (6)
Echelford Primary School

WHAT'S HAPPENING TO ME?

I ate some cheese and then I sneezed.
I ate a cake and began to shake.
I ate a kipper and started to shiver.
What's happening to me?

I drank some juice
I saw a goose.
I drank some tea
I smelled the sea.
I drank some Fanta
I thought I heard Santa!
What's happening to me?

Jessica Brown (8)
Echelford Primary School

WHEN I GROW UP!

When I grow up I shall be,
A sailor on the deep blue sea.
A sailor might get in a fight,
So I would not fancy that.

I could try to fly up high,
Upon a pigeon's back.
Or maybe not, knowing them
They'd rather take my snack.

I could be a singer,
Or a movie star.
I could have a scooter
And motor car!

If I get married
I shall marry a millionaire.
I could marry him for money,
I think that's rather funny.

Megan McGee (10)
Echelford Primary School

THE EAGLE

Beak as sharp as a razor,
Houses below like tiny specks.
Zooming so fast, the trees are a blur
The eagle, still flying, he's in a hex.

Claws like a knife and fork
For ripping up his prey,
Swooping down on it
In the month of May.

Cassie Garland (9)
Echelford Primary School

THE BAT

Swooping and gliding
In the moonlit sky
Staring down
As the world goes by.

Always listening like an owl
For any bug to eat
Fingers like swords has the bat
To find some juicy bug meat.

Everything like a splodge of paint
He flies as fast as a cheetah running
With his wings straight out
A bat can be very cunning.

He uses radar sonar
To track down his prey
All this technology in his body
He does all this every day.

Joel Smith (8)
Echelford Primary School

SPACE WALKING

Walking in space, walking on air, gravity free.
Planets, red, blue, orange and green.
Living on a planet crumbly and hard,
No friend, birthday or Christmas card!
Finding spacemen in rocky caves.
When I find them they give me waves.
Floating, living, life is a chase
All these things I did while walking in space.

Sian Williams (8)
Echelford Primary School

JUNK

Junk is what people throw away,
When they don't need it anymore.
It is dirty, smelly and rotten!
So most people just throw it on the floor.

It litters the city, the country, the world!
It is made out of old bits and bobs,
Stuff like paper, broken pencils
And old clothes, wrappers, yucky food
And doorknobs.

Our planet is overrun with things like these.
We should get rid of this stuff and start anew.
But most of the people that pollute the Earth
Could just one of these people be
        You?

Dani Curbie & Freyja McKenna (10)
Echelford Primary School

A CAT

Glowing eyes as bright as the sun,
Has the cat.
Ever so uscful to spot a rat.

Claws like sharp teeth
To scratch the rat.
Sitting on the fluffy mat.

Purrs like a motor
When she is stroked.
She thinks the motor's broken.

Ipek Balcik (8)
Echelford Primary School

BAGS

A busy man's briefcase hanging in his hand
Containing bills, mobile phone,
Forms, pens.

A lady's red handbag
Hanging on her arm
Containing, lipstick, hairbrush,
Make-up and a ring.

A sensible girl's bag
Sitting in her locker
Containing her reading wallet,
Homework and a pencil case.

A silly boy's school bag
Sitting on his back
Containing a catapult,
Chewing gum, apple core and a
Water gun.

Callie Gregory (8)
Echelford Primary School

CATS

Claws like a razor
Ready to rip my blazer
When the cat runs by he seeks
The moon night sky.
Fur as black as a witch's hat.
His whiskers are like white string.
When he sees a wing,
You hear his bell ping.

William Lewis (8)
Echelford Primary School

A Day At School

As the bell rings for the start of the day,
We all wish that we could stay and play.

'Stop talking' say the prefects when we walk up the stairs,
'Oh yeah and walk in pairs.'

And what did the teacher shout?
'Sit down and get your books out.'
Now it's time for the worst subject of the term,
That's maths where all we do is learn!

Lunchtime

As I run for the best seat,
All I see is meat!

After lunch we return to our rooms,
And then learn about the Egyptian tombs.

Now the bell rings for the end of the day,
And we are now free to play.

Jack Budd (9)
Echelford Primary School

Secret Life Of Old Toys

Many of our children know,
That as soon as they go to sleep,
The toys in their bedroom come to life
And slowly start to peep.

The teddy bears have a picnic,
With sandwiches and crisps galore.
All the other toys will gather around,
Every single toy you would adore.

As morning time creeps closer,
The toys go back to bed,
Your favourite teddy will snuggle up
And rest against your head.

Christopher Mertens (8)
Echelford Primary School

THE SHARK

Like a tiger of the sea
Waiting for an ambush
Searching in the coral
And in the seaweed mush.

Fins like wings on a torpedo
A tail moving with such strength
A predator, a carnivore
The fish with the longest tail length.

He swims with such accuracy
He has no claws
He stalks, he creeps
Then he catches with his jaws.

He uses radar sonar
To track down his prey
All of this technology he has inside his body
He does all this every day.

Imran Bhaluani (9)
Echelford Primary School

BOOKS

An information book from Ibiza
Sitting on its shelf
Containing animals, places, habitats,
Temperature and health.

A story book from Spain
Sitting on its shelf
Containing Cinderella, Snow White,
Little Red Riding Hood
And a story about an elf.

A poem book from Peru
Sitting on its shelf
Containing story poems and listing poems
Written all by myself.

Lucy Alker (9)
Echelford Primary School

THE BUTTERFLY

How huge is everything to a tiny butterfly.
How big is everything out here.
The sea feels like a million miles
And the sea is as colourful as me.

A bird is my enemy
It chases me like mad.
When I see a bird,
I fly as fast as the wind.

Leesa Richardson (8)
Echelford Primary School

THE LEOPARD

The leopard runs as fast as the wind
on the green grass.
His eyes sees a brown bunny.
He likes his food and eats meat just like he runs.
His eyes are like a night in the dark sky.
His fur is like yellow bananas.

Emily Smith (8)
Echelford Primary School

LONDON TOWN

London is the place I live,
It's big and bright and very loud.
With traffic going back and forth,
With sights galore to greet the eyes.
Tower Bridge, the Millennium Eye,
Tower of London, with jewels so bright.
The colours and smells of London town
Is what brings visitors all year round.
Its history of years gone by.
The Houses of Parliament, where laws are made.
The best place to see it all,
Is to take yourself along the mighty River Thames
where craft ply up and down.
Underneath its many bridges,
Which at night is a wonderful sight.

Nicola Malpass (8)
Edgware Junior School

MURDER IN THE MANOR

There stood the manor
Right on the hill
In that dead village
Lived Miss Tribill.

She was thirty five
With no family.
She grieved for them,
Very longingly.

Our story starts
On a dark gloomy night.
There was a shadow
Just one person in sight.

The murderer was cunning,
The murderer was fast,
He came in the empty house,
When midnight had passed.

He killed her with one stab,
One blow of the knife
He once loved her,
As she was his wife.

She died with a scream
She dropped right away.
But he stayed with her
'Til the break of day.

She's still lying there,
All alone in her house,
Nobody grieving for her,
The house is like a mouse.

Nobody knew her
Nobody cared,
Nobody loved her,
Nobody dared.

Aarti Dalsania (10) & Nabila Kazi (11)
Edgware Junior School

SPRINGFIELD SIMPSONS' POEM

Milhouse likes the kwik mark,
He's got a friend called Bart.

Bart likes to ride his skateboard
Nelson's seen a tiger who roared.

Lisa plays the saxophone,
Homer likes to moan and groan.

Barney always drinks beer
Marge says 'Oh dear!'

Flanders says 'Oh diddly do'
Homer says 'Oh quiet that bubbly joo.'

Marge says 'Are there any Rons?'
Ain't we The Simpsons?

Yes we are.
Oh naaaa.

Masih (8)
Edgware Junior School

THE SCARY TEACHER

My teacher is scary
And she's very hairy.
Whenever she's out
She always shouts.

My teacher is rude
When she's in a bad mood.
And sometimes she's mean
Then she turns green.

My teacher is warty
And she's naughty.
But when she's on the bus
She doesn't make a big fuss.

My teacher turns blue
When she has the flu.
But when she's on the train
She never, ever uses her brain.
My teacher is just plain scary!

Sayrah Malik (9)
Edgware Junior School

I SAW A JOLLY SNOWMAN

I saw a jolly snowman,
Made of jolly snow
Who had a jolly scarf
In the jolly show.

In the jolly show,
We had a jolly clap
People looking at jolly snowmen,
With a jolly slap.

On the jolly way,
People jolly go
Wearing a jolly scarf,
In the jolly snow.

Kanza Saleem (7)
Edgware Junior School

CHRISTMAS THANK YOUS

Dear Auntie,
Oh what a nice jumper,
I've always adored powder blue.
And fancy you thinking of orange and pink,
For the stripes,
How very clever of you!
Dear Gran,
Many thanks for the hankies,
Now I really can't wait for the flu,
And daisies embroidered in red round the 'S' for Shivani,
How very thoughtful of you!
Dear Uncle,
The soap is terrific, so useful and such a kind thought,
And how did you guess that I'd used the last of the soap,
The last Christmas bought!
Dear Cousin,
What socks! And the same sort you wear,
So you must be the last word in style
These socks will make me stand out a mile!
Dear Grandad,
Don't fret I'm delighted,
So don't think your gift will offend
Even though I've only got a fiver to spend!

Shivani Kumer (7)
Edgware Junior School

CLEAN IT UP!

Clean it up, clean it up,
All the litter should go in the bin,
Clean it up, clean it up.
Always think of the green metal tin.
Clean it up, clean it up,
All the trash goes flip, flop, tick, tock in the bin,
Clean it up, clean it up,
Flick rubbish in the bin,
Clean it up, clean it up,
Even if it's not yours, flick it in the bin,
Clean it up, clean it up,
Always dream to put your rubbish in the
Green metal bin,
Clean it up, clean it up,
Help Britain and let the cleaning begin.

Chandani Vishram (8)
Edgware Junior School

I SAW A JOLLY SNOWMAN

I saw a jolly snowman
Made of jolly snow
Who had a jolly show
In the jolly snow.

In the jolly show
He had a jolly clap
People looking at the snowman
With a jolly clap.

On the jolly way,
People jolly go
Wearing a long scarf,
After a while people jolly shout
In the jolly snow.

Damilola Oyenuga (8)
Edgware Junior School

TWO LITTLE KITTENS

Two little kittens
One stormy night
Began to quarrel
And then to fight.

One had a mouse
And the other had none;
And that was the way
The quarrel begun.

'I'll have that mouse'
Said the bigger cat.
'You'll have that mouse?
We'll see about that!'

'I will have that mouse!'
Said the tortoiseshell;
And, spitting and scratching
On her sister she yell.

I've told you before
'Twas a stormy night,
When these two kittens
Began to fight.

Genevieve Etienne-Farrell (7)
Edgware Junior School

SEASONS

Seasons come and seasons go
In winter there is sometimes snow
In spring the buds are on the trees
And I feel very, very pleased.
In summer it can get quite hot
Sometimes it rains and sometimes not
In autumn, leaves are brown and red
And end up looking like they're dead.
Another year has gone right past
And it has happened very fast
I wonder what this year will bring
In summer, autumn, winter, spring.

Emily Adkins (8)
Edgware Junior School

PAINT ON MY FINGERS

I banged a nail,
I hit my thumb,
My brother laughed,
But not my mum.
My brother tried,
To paint a face,
The paint went splattering
On his face,
He turned around,
And started to cry,
My mummy laughed, and so did I.

Alaa Alfadhli (8)
Edgware Junior School

MY INSIDES

Sometimes my brain
Wonders far away,
In France, Germany and Spain
And sometimes I really wish I was out to play.

Sometimes my tummy
Growls and rumbles
When I smell jelly
And apple crumble.

Sometimes my heart beats very fast
Very fast indeed
Pumping all the blood I need
Shouting through my veins in a blast.

Youssef Djeraoui (8)
Edgware Junior School

THE DAY THE ALIENS CAME TO EARTH

The day the aliens came to Earth,
They came to take over human birth.
They got the children, the poor souls,
And took them away to eat them whole.
We won, we won, we won they sang,
And then there was a real big bang.
The army was tough they were really on,
They fought and they fought till they thought
They were gone.
The next day they went away,
And never came back, that's what they say.

Fela Latilo (9)
Edgware Junior School

FASTER, HIGHER, STRONGER

'Faster, higher, stronger,'
Is the motto we are told,
But how do our Olympics
Compare with times of old?

On the slope of Mount Olympus
One thousand years BC
The Ancient Greeks competed
For their gods above to see.

Each strove to be a winner
Of the sprint, the one big race,
And wrestled, boxed or chariot-raced,
To gain a prized first place.

They were given no gold medals
Or trophies to display,
But all their great achievements,
Were talked of miles away.

In this new millennium,
The tradition carries on.
From one hundred and twenty nations,
Come seven thousand strong.

The lighting of the Olympic torch
Links us with times past.
While with modern high technology
Instant pictures are broadcast.

Many are disappointed,
After the excitement of the start,
But there's no disgrace in losing,
Only pride in taking part.

Amy Mayles (11)
Edgware Junior School

CHILDREN

Hair
Black hair
Brown hair
Long hair
Short hair
Light hair
Dark hair.

Hands
Small hands
Big hands
Dirty hands
Clean hands
Wrinkled hands
Soft hands.

Eyes
Green eyes
Blue eyes
Big eyes
Small eyes
Dark eyes
Bright eyes.

Feet
Nice feet
Horrible feet
Smelly feet
Sweet feet
Dirty feet
Clean feet.

Jade Dabare (9)
Edgware Junior School

HEROES, HEROINES AND MONSTERS

Heroes and heroines may rise to fame,
They are the people who always save the day.
Gods and goddesses give them help,
Their power and greatness can be felt.
Heroes and heroines are found all over the world,
They can even be a boy or girl.
When monsters scare you and make you cry,
But in the end, they must die.
Killed by the powers of the heroes might,
Monsters can never defeat them in a fight.
Monsters, may appear,
Anytime, any place, anywhere.
They may look like dragons and breathe out smoke,
But to heroes and heroines they are just a joke.
They can't harm them anyway,
So once again they'll save the day.
The monster could be a gigantic cat,
Or it could be a dragon that flies like a bat.
When they cut off its great big head,
Once again the monster is dead.
No point fighting, they know who wins,
It would either be the hero or the heroine.
So, beware of the mythical figure you see,
You never know what it might be?

Vasroy Fuller (10)
Edgware Junior School

SWEETS

I love sweets, any kind of sweet.
Short ones, long ones, small ones, round ones,
Thin ones, any shape ones.
I lick them, I bite them, I crunch them,
I munch them, I eat them all.
But then I have to go to the dentist
Who puts me in the big black chair
And says to me 'This one has to go,
And that one and that one.'
'Oh no' says Mum.

Shanika Douglas (8)
Edgware Junior School

FACING UP TO MY ENEMY

I left the shop and began to roam,
But after a while I rambled home.
I saw my enemy in front of the house,
As soon as I saw it I felt like a mouse.

I tip-toed up the drive as quietly as could be.
My enemy's eyes always following me.
My head was buzzing, I felt trapped,
Forced from home by the neighbour's cat!

I gave a deep breath and tried to feel brave,
As I gradually approached this cat called 'Dave'.
Suddenly I received a brainwave
Thought of something to attack.

Taking out a bottle of mineral water . . .
I hurled it at that cat!

Neha Thakrar (10)
Holland House School

THE UNUSUAL ELEPHANT

Bump! went the elephant,
As he landed on the floor.
He had tried to climb a tree,
And now his back was sore.

He started to see stars,
That circled round and round.
He got up and tried to walk,
But he fell back to the ground.

When he woke up from his slumber,
He walked back to the tree.
He clamped his legs around it,
The birds away did flee.

Further up he climbed the tree,
Until he reached the top.
He picked a ripe banana,
And ate it with a slip and a slop!

The unsteady tree started to swing and sway,
Still the elephant tried to hold on.
But he lost his grip at the top of the tree,
And his life as a monkey had gone.

For one last time he landed with a plop!
And again his back was sore.
But the elephant knew his place in the world,
Was firmly upon the floor.

Daniel Rothman (11)
Holland House School

THE PURR

He'll stalk you,
But when you look down upon him,
His huge round eyes,
Will plead with you.
And then it starts.
That magical sound
Which conquers and softens all hearts
    The purr.

You'll pick him up
To feel that rumbling sensation
Tickling your hands
And you'll think
'There could never be a cat more loving
than you . . . oh!'
His claws are kneading you,
And when he catches your eye this way,
You know he'll be your friend forever,
With that ever echoing purr.

When you place him on your lap,
Seated on the sofa,
His huge round eyes will start to close,
Into tiny amber slits.
Your eyes slowly will close too,
And together you will travel to Nod.
Still with that magical sound
    The purr.

Charlotte Allen (11)
Holland House School

WHAT IF?

What if sky was green?
What if grass was blue?
What if fish could fly?
What if birds could swim?
What would it be like if life was like this?

What if animals could talk?
What if humans could not?
What if he was she?
What if she was he?
What would it be like if life was like this?

What if night was day?
What if light was dark?
What if black was white?
What if backwards was forwards?
What would it be like if life was like this?

What if arms were legs?
What if hands were feet?
What if fingers were toes?
What if front was back?
What would it be like if life was like this?

What if wide was narrow?
What if long was short?
What if life was death?
What if good was bad?
What would it be like if life was like this?

Would all this be right?
Would all this be wrong?
And would it really matter if life was like this?

Ashley Moss (11)
Holland House School

A PAINFUL LANGUAGE

Vain, Vane, Vein,
English is a pain
Although the words sound alike
The spellings not the same!

Bee, Be, B
I'd rather climb a tree
There are some words we have to learn
Not one but three!

Right, Rite, Write
I'd rather be cheering on a fight
Not struggling with all my might
To grasp the silent letters to write!

Cite, Sight, Site
I'd rather be the light
Looking down upon the children
Learning this painful language!

Too, To, Two
I'd rather catch flu
Lying in my bed
Not learning the stressful language!

Their, There, They're
It isn't really fair
This is a beautiful language
But much too hard to learn and spell!

Sagar Shah (11)
Holland House School

The New Dish

Under the sea a restaurant lies
Filled with bread, cakes and pies.
Mr Chunt owns this place,
But not once has a face,
Entered this shop to buy some food
Not one meal has been eaten or chewed.

Mr Chunt had no money
Other fish thought it was funny,
That Mr Chunt would never shut
His lonely shop, his lonely hut.
But Mr Chunt would not stop
He wanted his restaurant to be the top.

One day Mr Chunt had an idea.
He mixed some wine, he mixed some beer,
He added seaweed and coral too,
And chewing gum which he had to chew.
Before he put them together
And stirred them with a seagull's feather.

The next day he opened the shop,
And before long it was the top!
Every fin and every tail
Crowded in with every whale
And every shark and every fish
Pushed each other to taste the dish.

Five hours later the last fish departed
And this is where Mr Chunt started
Chewing on the final slice
The party was over - and it had been nice.

But the end of the story has been said:
When Mr Chunt woke up in bed.

Sam Pinner (10)
Holland House School

THE PLANETARY RHYME

Mercury is first and nearest to the sun
Its very own word is my.

Venus is hot on second
With its word very upon the trail.

The Earth, our dwelling, is third
Excellent just happens to be its word

Red old Mars is coming fourth
Has the word Mother for itself.

Fifth is Jupiter largest of them all
Lies at an angle that just is standing tall.

Saturn is sliding in sixth
Its circling rings make a shroud for showed.

Uranus with its letters first and last
Is seventh and provides the word us.

Neptune comes eighth
One from last but its word is nine.

Small Pluto comes in ninth and last
Puts the word planets at its end.

Now you have heard my rhyme
To place them in order it is time
'My very excellent Mother just showed us nine planets.'

Anthony Chaplin (10)
Holland House School

MYSTERY

Sometimes it's fear,
Other times it's excitement,
Never expected,
And always unknown.

Around every corner,
Lurks suspense,
The mystery is always with you,
Never leaving you alone.

Goosebumps bulge,
A shiver shoots down your spine
Like a bullet from a gun
As the tension builds and nerves act up.

The wind flows through your hair,
And the perspiration stops,
The drumming of your heart
becomes a faint knock on the door
And your lungs relax as you calm down.

All this happens
As the secret is revealed,
But mysteries are always building
And ever lurking around each movement of life.

Karim Javeri (11)
Holland House School

THE FLOOD

The banks suddenly burst,
After days of heavy rain.
Everyone was all a flurry,
My world could never be the same.

My favourite bridge across the river
I could not see it through the door.
It had been swallowed by the brook
Until it was there no more.

The water flashed in a torrent
Passing my window as I look out.
The drops of water upon the glass
Are dancing all about.

The drops dribbled down the pane
Having finally finished their dance.
As they were preparing to die on the window sill
They gave me a sorrowful glance.

Amy Lerman (11)
Holland House School

SEASONS

I glare out my window and I see the sun
Like a hot steaming burger in its bun.
I glare out of my window
and I see golden brown leaves crunching like brittle glass.
I glare out of my window and I see diamond white grass.

I glare out of my window
and I see blossom that smells as sweet as a rose.

Melissa Leigh (8)
Rosh Pinah Primary School

Stay In The Future

A darkened day, a stormy night
Just awes winter's numinous might.

A cloudy raft of snow and sleet
Listening to sad sheep baa and bleat.

This stormy night on a winter's day
Just proves what autumn threw away
The leaves would fall at dawn of day
And in them kids would laugh and play.

Autumn but was a clichè
Singularly compared with a summer's day.

The sun would shine through cloud and cloud
And people would gather to cheer and crowd.

But in spring there was no crowd
But time to sit with muted sound
Time to stay from present and past
Just stay in future vast!

Benjamin Deaner (9)
Rosh Pinah Primary School

Seasons

Here comes spring,
When the trees blossom,
Pink, yellow, purple, blue,
Then spring rain comes
Trees and flowers grow too.

Summer is starting,
The trees are healthy
With all their leaves
And a slight breeze.

It is time for autumn,
When all the leaves fall.
When the leaves turn gold,
Which can easily fold.

Winter is finally here,
The trees are all bare.
With snow instead of leaves,
The grass has all froze.

Florence Schechter (9)
Rosh Pinah Primary School

FIREWORKS

It was a cold winter's night
and the moon was shining bright.
We are going to a firework display tonight.
We know that it will be just right.

The fireworks gave a bang
It was like an orchestra that sang.
The rockets shot up towards the sky
And then I heard a little boy cry.

The fireworks were happening in two places
It looked like they were having races.
The fireworks were going up high and wide
I'm glad my Dad was by my side.

There were lots of people there
All we could do was stare.
We gathered in pairs
And sat together on the chairs.
And in the end it was a lot of fun.

Dalia Coleman (10)
Rosh Pinah Primary School

TU BISHEVAT

Tu Bishevat 1

Tu Bishevat is coming,
There's one more week to go.
I wish it was here now,
So I wouldn't feel so low.
We eat lovely pears and apples,
Grapes and oranges too.
Unfortunately this year's Schmitta,
We can't even grow one tree!

Tu Bishevat 2

Tu Bishevat is here,
Under trees
Bananas grow
Say, do you want an apple?
Hey! They taste brilliant you know,
Everybody loves them
Very, very much.
All of us have to go now,
Ta ta, see you next year.

Abbie Mandel
Rosh Pinah Primary School

STANDING TREE

There was a tree which stood in the garden.
In winter it was blown by strong winds
In spring the tree blossomed.
In summer the leaves are bright and green
And in autumn the leaves turn red and gold and fall off the tree.

There was a tree which stood in a garden
In winter the winds were even stronger than last year.
In spring the tree blossomed even more than last year
In summer the tree had even more leaves on than last year
And in autumn, even more leaves fell than last year.

Rebecca Laster (9)
Rosh Pinah Primary School

POTATOES

There are different kinds of potatoes,
There are nine that you can find,
Big ones, small ones, fat and thin ones,
I'll put them in your mind.

Alpha, Roseval, Timate,
Mini and Dita,
Clauster, Bakers,
Nicola and Flea.

The American chef, George Crumb,
Was serving French fries,
Then a Frenchman came in,
What a surprise!

He served his customer
His enormous portion,
But he wanted it fried more,
In faster motion.

So he fried these again and again,
And served it to all the men,
Without knowing it, he had made crisps.
Out of chips!

Sara Kandler (10)
Rosh Pinah Primary School

SPACE

I look out of my window,
And up into the sky,
Millions of stars,
All shimmering in my eye.

I notice planets,
Much nearer than the stars,
Jupiter is red,
The same as Mars.

I see the moon,
Glimmering white,
Coloured from
The sun's light.

Then there is Mercury,
And Venus too,
Who spin round the sun,
Faster than when you flush the loo.

The outer planets,
Are made of gas,
And because of this,
They have a small mass.

The sun is also,
Made of gas.
But because it is bigger,
It has a much larger mass.

But one day,
There will be a big bash,
And the planets will be swallowed up,
In a big mash.

Saul Freedman (10)
Rosh Pinah Primary School

FRUITS I LIKE

The red rosy apple is a delight
If you want you can eat it at night.
What you do with it is your choice
My hands are all moisty before I eat.
My face is burning with heat
Because I just want that munch
So badly I could punch.

A crispy Le Crunch
Is nice to munch
And the crunch is unbearable to see
So what can I say I have to have
It everyday.

The slimy slick banana is yellow like the sun.
Its skin is thin and scaly you could slip on it
Which would be embarrassing.

The pear is green
And of course it is so clean.
It is a very dull colour but it's so scrumptious
When you take a munch.

The orange is lovely and ripe
It is a different sort of fruit
Because it is so sweet like sugar.

Penina Ford (9)
Rosh Pinah Primary School

117

CHOCOLATE MOUSSE

Chocolate mousse, chocolate mousse,
Chocolate mousse is lovely and loose.
Chocolate mousse may look horrible and brown,
But really it is lovely as the mousse goes down.
As chocolate mousse goes down your tummy,
It gets extremely yummy and scrummy.
As the smell goes up your nose,
It opens its brown mouth and goes
'I know I may look horrible but really I am not,
Believe me I taste good! Lovely scrummy and hot.'
So eat chocolate mousse it's like your best mate,
And eat chocolate mousse because it's really, really *great!*

Sophie Truman (10)
Rosh Pinah Primary School

FLOWERS

In England you can plant a sunflower in summer.
A daffodil in spring,
And all the birds will come out and sing.

Some flowers grow on trees,
Some flowers grow from seeds.
Most of all they're always there,
To help you smell the fresh air.

Queen Elizabeth kept a flower under her nose,
To stop the smell of smelly toes.

Flowers always like to show,
With rain and sun they grow and grow.

Emma Kingston (10)
Rosh Pinah Primary School

THE GREAT OAK TREE

In the middle of my garden stands tall and strong
A great oak tree.
The great oak tree is said to have stood firm
And still on the lawn for millions of years.
I gaze upon it from my window and wonder,
I wonder what it is like for the sparrow
That is perched on the tree's highest branch.
Sleeping in her nest.
My great oak tree lets me swing on its low strong boughs.
Whilst I speak to him, and he seems to talk back,
With the rustling of his dark green leaves.
Just like an old friend.

Alexander Gordon (10)
Rosh Pinah Primary School

THE SEASONS

The seasons come, the seasons go
This is something we all know

In winter it is very cold
To go outside is very bold

To clean the house of dirty things
Is what Mummy does in the spring

Summer days are long and hot
We have time to play a lot

Autumn days are getting shorter
And the trees are getting balder.

Nicholas Simons (8)
Rosh Pinah Primary School

TV

Flick, flick, flicker,
through all the channels you can find,
staring at the TV,
you can never stop,
nearer or sooner your head will go pop,
scary, spooky, weird and wonkers,
sometimes your mum will go bonkers.

Football channel must jump up,
you're so caught up, you can crack a nut.

Music channel must dance around,
sometimes you can never be found.

Everyone has to watch it,
if they have a TV or not!

It's great to see,
and great to feel,
so loveable about the TV!

Talia Houri (10)
Rosh Pinah Primary School

THE SOLAR SYSTEM

The Earth revolves around the sun
Like a small piece of gum.
The solar system is so big,
It's even bigger than a giant oil rig.
You can see the bright stars
From red-hot Mars
And the other planets in the solar system.

The biggest star, the sun is so bright,
To make up for it you will need a billion torchlights.
In the sky are shooting stars,
If one hits you, you'll get sent off to sunny Mars.

Sam Potashnick (10)
Rosh Pinah Primary School

ALL THE FOUR SEASONS

Spring
In spring all the lambs are born and all the little calves are born,
In the spring plants start to grow again.
Daffodils and tulips grow.
The blossom also grows on the tree.
Joey, my tortoise, wakes up from his winter sleep.

Summer
In the summer it is the hottest part of the year.
Blossom grows into fruit on the trees.
The schools have finished and people go on holidays.

Autumn
In autumn, leaves fall off the trees,
Only evergreen trees stay with green leaves.
And it starts to get colder.

Winter
Winter is the coldest part of the year.
It snows a lot and there is frost on the cars.
Joey goes into his box for the winter.
All the trees are bare.

Summer is my favourite time of the year
Because I love playing outdoors.

Daniella Colletts (8)
Rosh Pinah Primary School

JELLY

Jelly is yummy as it wobbles down my tummy.
Blue jelly, yellow jelly, red jelly, green,
I don't even care if it's made of a bean.
Carrot jelly, tomato jelly, broccoli jelly, lentil,
Sometimes when I eat it, I think I'm going mental.
Second helping, third helping, fourth helping, fifth,
When I eat too much it seems like a myth.
Bubbly jelly, smooth jelly, thin jelly, thick,
When I eat a lot of it, I sometimes feel quite sick.
Apple jelly, orange jelly, cherry jelly, plum.
While I eat my jelly my hands go numb.
Cheese jelly, butter jelly, jam jelly, honey
Eat it in the morning and your whole day will be sunny.
Aqua jelly, lime jelly, purple jelly, pink
Pink is my favourite to eat in a wink.

Alexa Jacobs (9)
Rosh Pinah Primary School

WHY ARE THE LEAVES BROWN?

Why are the leaves brown Mummy?
Because it's nearly Autumn.
Why are the leaves brown Mummy?
Because winter is near.
Why are the leaves brown Mummy?
Because it's nearly spring.
Why are the blossoms pink Mummy?
Because summer is near.
Why are the leaves green Mummy?
Because summer is here.
Why are the leaves brown Mummy?
Because it's nearly autumn.

Jamie Solomons (9)
Rosh Pinah Primary School

SUMMER AT THE BEACH

In the warm golden sand as people lay,
Some children swim while others play.
Happy moments being captured on film,
Some people jump out of the water, some jump in.
People eating in a happy mood,
Seagulls scoop searching for scraps of food.
Ice creams melting in the summer heat
Children hop on the sand with burning feet.
High up in the sky the sun shines bright,
The tide crashes down to a foamy white.
Footprints in the sand disappear,
Washed away by the tide that's coming near.
The sun is now setting, people pack to go home,
The beach is now deserted, and all alone.

Kate Mordecai (9)
Rosh Pinah Primary School

THE FLOWERS IN MY GARDEN

When it is spring the flowers start to grow and blossom.
The colours, pink, yellow, purple, red and orange
are the colours of the blossom on the trees.

When it is summer the bees are out, buzzing about in the flowers.

When it is autumn the leaves start to fall off the branches,
the leaves turn golden and red.

When it's winter, it starts to snow and all the plants die.

But when it's spring again it's a time of joy and laughter
For when the butterflies fly around the sky.

Abigail Glass (8)
Rosh Pinah Primary School

MY CAT POSSOM

Her name was Possom, silk white and shiny, she understands me,
She was as white as the walls on a sunny day
She was so cute as a first born kitten.
We gave her food upon a china plate,
Her favourite was chicken.
She was a hero
She protected the innocent from the enemy.

When we stroked her she purred,
But words cannot describe how I felt when
She slept with me, purring away.

Now she's no longer with us
I know she's at rest
Her photos are by my side
I will never forget her
Because she was the very best.

David Burns (10)
Rosh Pinah Primary School

IN THE WINTER'S BREEZE

It's time for the robin to start its winter
Time for him to sing a little song
On this glittering tree
In the winter's breeze.

Jumping from wall to wall
Standing on the leaves
While they turn to brittle glass,
In the winter's breeze.

Tweet, tweet he chanted
Singing his little song
While the animals are asleep
In the winter's breeze.

Michaela Jeffries (8)
Rosh Pinah Primary School

SPRING TO SUMMER TO AUTUMN TO WINTER

Spring is blossom,
Spring is fun,
Summer finishes spring,
Summer brings its wings.
Spring is great
Summer is better.
Autumn finishes summer,
Spring gives blossom up on the trees.
Summer gives sun to everyone,
Spring starts summer,
Summer and spring,
Winter ends autumn,
Autumn ends summer,
Winter is cold,
Colder than before,
Winter freezes the trees,
It freezes our hands and feet
Even toes and fingers,
But to me ice is colder.

Lana Rose Moses (8)
Rosh Pinah Primary School

Trees Live Or Die

As time flies by
Trees live or die.
In spring the trees
Start to grow.
In summer they
glow at sight.
In autumn the
leaves change colour
and start to fall.
In winter trees
say goodbye
to their friends and nests.
As time flies by
Trees live or die.
Why do trees die?
How can trees live?
How do they live? How do they die?
As time flies by
Trees live or die.

Nicole Dallal (8)
Rosh Pinah Primary School

There's A Robin In My Garden

There's a robin in my garden
Chirping through the season
Hopping on the icy wall
Fluttering for no reason.

The little robin redbreast
Searching round for food
Looking under tables
In an unhappy mood.

When autumn comes around
The little robin's fine
Laying in its wooden nest
Waiting for a sign.

Monica Leverton (9)
Rosh Pinah Primary School

THE SEASONS FLOW BY

Ladies and gentlemen
Please may I have your attention.

Spring's here,
There's nothing to fear.
Blossoms grow on trees,
And nectar gets taken by bees.

Summer's here,
There's nothing to fear.
Under the blazing sun,
Is where children have fun.

Autumn's here,
There's nothing to fear.
Leaves start to fall,
The beginning of football.

Winter's here,
There's nothing to fear.
Droppings of white in the snow,
Soon the snow will go, go, go.

And the birds will fly,
As the seasons flow by.

Daniel Beitler (9)
Rosh Pinah Primary School

THE SEASONS

Now, summer has come and spring has gone
The sun is shining and the birds are gliding
Children are playing hide and seek
And the adults are telling them not to peek!
While the other children play with a bunny
The hard-working bees are all making honey
Now it's autumn the leaves are falling
And the weather is starting to get quite appalling.
When they fall to the ground they turn, gold,
                                        brown or red.
It looks like the leaves have made a small leaf bed!
Soon it turns winter, the snowflakes fall.
It's really too cold to play outside with a ball.
A few weeks later it will turn to spring
The flowers will blossom and the birds will sing
The children are playing hide and seek
And the adults are telling them not to peek!
Soon it will be summer again.

Katrina Jascourt (9)
Rosh Pinah Primary School

HOW A FLOWER GROWS

In spring Mum planted a flower
Then in summer it got bigger
And bigger, and bigger, and bigger!
But then in the autumn the blooms fell,
And fell, and fell, and fell!
In the winter the plant froze
And froze, and froze, and froze!

Joel Rosenthal (9)
Rosh Pinah Primary School

HOW DO TREES SURVIVE

As time flies by
Trees their leaves
Turn into gold
Leaves start jumping
Onto the ground
Suddenly the leaves
Begin to grow on the
Trees and blossoms
Comes out all pretty
Some are pink and
Some are yellow.
Now it's autumn
It's time for the leaves to fall.
They turn into brown
Then orange then
Gold.

Hope Allsuch (8)
Rosh Pinah Primary School

A TREE CHANGE

In the spring the trees are dark green,
They are covered in blossom.
Now it's summer and at the end,
They will start to fall and
Change colour.
Now it's autumn
The leaves are golden brown,
It's winter and it's very cold,
When they touch the ground,
They will be brittle as glass.

Benjamin Gordon (9)
Rosh Pinah Primary School

MY LITTLE FLOWER

My little flower
Is sleeping at the moment
And the soil is as solid
As dry cement.

My little flower
Has become as bad
And now the soil
Is just like mud.

My little flower
Is as beautiful as can be
And the soil
Is as gentle as the sea.

My little flower
Is dying in the sky
And I have to wait so long
For my flower to bloom again.

But why?

Nicole Melzack (9)
Rosh Pinah Primary School

THE SEASON RATS

In the season winter, the little rat would shiver
In the season spring, the little rat would sing
In the season summer, the little rat would feel lazy and sleepy
In the season autumn, the little rat would hold a big feast
to round off the bumpy season.

Matthew Hertz (9)
Rosh Pinah Primary School

INTO A MOUSE HOLE

In a room
There was a house
And that house was
Of a mouse.

That entrance
Of the dirty hole,
Could it be,
A lump of coal?

By the hole
The nasty chap
The housekeeper put
A deadly mousetrap!

Here comes the mouse
Coming back from dinner
Dodging the trap, walks through the hole
The human wasn't the winner.

Over the water pipe
Through the shoe,
The mouse is going through its home
Now passing the loo.

He runs and runs
Around his home,
And soon sleeps in bed
All alone.

Reuven Shirazi (8)
Rosh Pinah Primary School

ALL FOUR SEASONS

Spring is hot,
but sometimes cold.
It brings the fun
to everyone.
People go out to play
to enjoy the day.
Everyone does not enjoy
Spring because summer
is more fun,
Because the sun shines more.
Winter is cold, it sometimes snows
When people are not there to see it.
It is cool but,
Winter is colder.
People love summer because they can go
on the beach to play on the sand and you.

Sarah Bennett (8)
Rosh Pinah Primary School

THE RAIN SEASONS

One of the four seasons
are down in the sun,
where you have lots
and lots of fun.

Yellow is the sun,
White is vanilla ice cream.
Brown is tea,
You don't have near here.
So be happy with me by the sea.

One of the four seasons is spring,
Where the birds spread out their wing.
The flowers all pretty pink,
Grass fresh green,
Blue is the sky,
And everybody's eating pie.

Sarah-Jayne Grahame (9)
Rosh Pinah Primary School

THE TALL TREE

I am a tree,
I am very large and green,
I have lots of leaves in the spring,
I am the tallest tree, I am like a king.

In the summer all the birds lay
Their nest upon my branch
In the morning of the day
My leaves change colour,
My branch becomes duller.

In the autumn, my leaves start to fall off
My branch.
I feel very cold and my leaves are gone
And when they are on the floor they get crunchy.

In the winter all the leaves have gone,
Snow forming on the branch, frost coming
Next, I can't wait until the summer and
The sun is gone.

Hilla Torbati (9)
Rosh Pinah Primary School

THE SEASONS

The seasons are good, the seasons are fun.
They are different for everyone.
Animals are good, animals are wicked,
Some are good, some are bad.
People are good, people are bad
They can be a really good dad,
For a son or a daughter, mothers as well.
Trees are good, leaves are gold and silver
Like the seasons of the year!

Spring is fresh, bright and breezy
Flowers growing very easy.

Summer is hot, summer is good,
You can play on the beach and that's good too.

Autumn is messy, autumn is good
All the leaves fall and the day is really cool.

Winter is cold, winter is freezing,
Winter is good for everyone.

As I look out the window I see it is snowing
I hope you liked reading my poem!

Nicholas Aronberg (6)
Rosh Pinah Primary School

THE JOURNEY OF THE TREES

The trees are very happy
In the summer,
And not in the winter.

There are no leaves in spring,
But beautiful pink leaves
And they are called blossoms.

And in the winter they look bare,
Just like they wanted to go to sleep and
Can't wait till summer.

All the trees will not get sunburnt.
And get very hot from way up high.
So the trees are very tired at the end of the day.

Adam Levy (9)
Rosh Pinah Primary School

MY LIFE AS A SEED

It was April the 1st in the spring
I was put on a flower bed
By a girl with a shiny, gold ring.
She gave me a cold shower
Then covered me with a pile of mud.
I think she was trying to keep me comfortable.

It was summer
I wanted to see light
So I shot up
And I was scared of heights
But I have a right
To do what I like.

It was autumn
I was fully grown
And I didn't moan
And that's the end of autumn.

It was winter
I collapsed in the flower bed
And the snow buried me
Like a tree falling on me.

Ilana Grossmark (8)
Rosh Pinah Primary School

FLOWER

My flower starts as a seed,
Some people think I'm a weed.
But when I am up,
The gardener is up and ready to feed me away.

The petals float,
Like a boat over the endless seas.
But in a way the petals fly
On the endless breeze.

Children pick me,
My petals fall off me.
And I go on the breeze,
But when I land on the signpost of Strand
That is the end of me.

The petals float,
Like a boat over the endless seas.
But in a way the petals fly,
On the endless breeze.

Benjamin Winton (9)
Rosh Pinah Primary School

RED ROSE

I am a tiny little bud,
Don't splash me with mud.
I grow as you water me,
Not as you talk to me.

I am a long stem
Just like a thin pen.
My petals come out,
All shining and bright.

I am ready for the summer,
It's all nice and hot.
People admire me,
But I'll look even better in a brown pot.

Jessica Moses (8)
Rosh Pinah Primary School

HOW THE BOAT SANK

The boat sails away
It has twelve people on board
The twelve people want to catch a shark
With a big long sword.

Here comes a shark
They catch it, what luck!
They see a chicken
And it goes cluck, cluck.

They have already caught six
They are having a dance
With can-can kicks
And big finger flicks.

Here comes the ninth
They say they do it for fame
I think it is greed
They will understand
When they get the blame.

Here comes number ten
The captain grabs it
With his hand
And smashes the boat.

Roei Samuel (9)
Rosh Pinah Primary School

ON A BLANKET OF GREEN GRASS

On a blanket of green grass
The farmer comes and plants a seed.

Deep underground
Where I'll be found,
There's everything you can imagine
Dark underground.

Bobbing up on the surface
Feeling fresh as air,
I was feeling sorry
For my old chaps down there.
It really is not fair!

Looking at the life around
It really did amaze me.
It was like going around
In the most amazing phase!

Nicholas Feingold (8)
Rosh Pinah Primary School

A SMASHING DAY WITH COMET!

A smashing comet is a bashing comet,
That hurls away from the sun.

With a *zoom* and a *boom* it would crash
And bash into pieces.
It flies around with a bounce and a pounce
Off every asteroid and meteorite.

It would smash and bash in its cloud of gas
And nearly hits trash that is left by the ships of space
By the human race.

Gideon Rothstein (9)
Rosh Pinah Primary School

A Fox's Daily Life

I get up in the morning
Into the chicken's farmyard
Eat a few chickens then I creep away
Then I have a quick run.
Then the farmers come, they chase me around
But they always slip up on the ground.

Every day I go in a bin
And that puts a happy grin
That's me happy, that's me with a farmer's hat.

At night-time I run through gardens
Then I sleep in a bin which smells worse than fish
But when I eat I always have a small dish.

Aaron Wunsh (8)
Rosh Pinah Primary School

The Season Hedgehog

In spring a little hedgehog was born
And he loved eating corn.
He's got the spikiest hair in town
But it doesn't make him frown.

In summer his spikes were small
And he was not very tall.

In autumn he started digging a hole
But not as fast as a mole.

In winter the hedgehog was in his hole
Trying to read a scroll.

Ariel Kamara
Rosh Pinah Primary School

THREE WHOLE MILES

We're walking;
Just walking
For three whole miles,
And we'll
Get for charity
Three pounds for every half a mile.
Three whole pounds!
Altogether,
That's eighteen pounds!
We'll give the money
To charity,
To help the poor people in India.
To help the homeless in India.
That terrible earthquake,
Killed tens of thousands of people.
So we're walking through the park,
The forest,
And back.
Right now we're passing the stream
As clear as crystal.
Trickling down the hill
We're really getting tired,
Walking up the hill
Nearly back.
I can't wait.
To get the money.
For the poor people in India.
For the homeless in India.
I've now walked three miles.
And raised another eighteen pounds for India.

David Shaw (9)
Rosh Pinah Primary School

MY LIFE AS A CAT

In spring
I like to sing
Sitting a ring
Then I saw a bird
Hopping its wings.
Sleep, sleep, creak, creak,
Go to catch a mouse,
Be back at eight, see you in the house.

In summer
I am so happy
Going swimming
Having ice cream
And dreaming
Eat baked beans.
Sleep, sleep, creak, creak,
Go to catch a mouse,
Be back at eight, see you in the house.

In autumn
I jump in the leaves
Have a laugh
It sounds daft
Sleep, sleep, creak, creak
Go to catch a mouse,
Be back at eight, see you in the house.

Sophie Sugarman (8)
Rosh Pinah Primary School

A Journey Through Trees

I am a little tree
All I ever do is look at all the blossom
I am a little tree
And all the flowers swing with me.

Now we are in the summer
And now it is much drier.
I am a little tree
And all the bees come on me.

Now we are in the autumn
But all the leaves fall down.
I am a little tree
And all the leaves fall on me.

Now we are in the winter
And all the rain falls on me
I am a little tree
And all the rain comes on me!

Amanda Daniels (9)
Rosh Pinah Primary School

Trees

I am an oak tree
Wide and awake
I like to shiver but not to shake
I don't like too many birds settling down on me
My branches will set me free.

I sit here in the summer
Winter, spring and autumn
Changing all the colours from dark to light,
And I like it when I'm shone very bright
From dark to light.

Sitting down here,
But there is no fear
Watching days and nights
And there is still no sight.

Myra Samra (8)
Rosh Pinah Primary School

BEAUTIFUL FLOWERS

I am a seed,
Ready to split
Waiting to be watered
And the sun to be lit.

I am stuck in the soil,
About to grow
My stem coming out,
With a bright green glow.

Leaves shooting out,
One by one,
Very strong and sturdy
I am nearly done.

Petals approaching
Red, yellow and white
Forming into a bed
Very secure and tight.

Slowly, slowly opening
What a pleasant sight
Lots and lots of colours,
In the bright sunlight.

Alex Benedyk (9)
Rosh Pinah Primary School

A Garden Through The Seasons

A garden in the spring
It is fresh
The flowers are at their best
The sky is blue
Even a bird flew through.

A garden in the summer
Is hot,
Also my flowers
And the trees die
Because they can't take the heat.

A garden in the autumn
Is bare
I can't really care
About my garden
And stare at my plants
I've planted through the year.

A garden in the winter
Is cold
A blanket of white snow
Covers me
And you can't see how pretty I can be.

Grace Dunsby (9)
Rosh Pinah Primary School

JOURNEY THROUGH SPACE

We're on a journey through space
We're on a journey past the sun,
We'll have to dodge planets
And the asteroid Zun.

We'll have to land on Zing
The planet next to Zun.
It's gonna be tough
But we'll have some fun.

We've just passed the sun
We're well on our way.
We're near Zing
So don't go away.

Here comes Zun
So be on your guard.
We'll explode the blighter
There, that wasn't so hard.

There's Zing
Our stop is near.
Don't fail rocket
Yee-ha, we're here.

Raphael Gray (9)
Rosh Pinah Primary School

HIBERNATION

Alas, it is spring again,
We need to get out of our burrows,
What a shame.

All we do in winter is,
Sleep in total blackness.
But now we have to work all day,
For the queen, our highness.

Maybe one day I'll be free
Always lively as a bee.

As all the days went by
The baby birds began to fly.

At last I have reached my destination,
Huddling down for hibernation.

Benjamin Fingerhut (9)
Rosh Pinah Primary School

LIFE OF A TREE FROM THE POINT OF ME

I am a tree.
My leaves bud in the spring
And fall off in the winter.
My leaves turn different colours
As the seasons go past.
In the spring I get my leaves when they blossom.
They are pink coloured and change colour in the summer.
They change to green in the summer
And change again in the autumn to brown.

Sarah Levy (8)
Rosh Pinah Primary School

THE LIFE OF A SEED

I am a little seed
I have just been planted
I'll fight off all the weeds
And help my other friends.

Now my stem is growing,
I'll soon be very big,
I'll have all different colours,
And grow lots of leaves.

Now I am a plant
I have lots of blossom.
And fruit and leaves
I've grown from one tiny seed.

Soon I will die
And lose my pretty blossom
I'll lose my fruit and leaves,
And go to a restless sleep.

Carmel Bergbaum (8)
Rosh Pinah Primary School

OUCH!

Sliding in the playground ouch!
Sliding for your Game Boy ouch!
Sliding with your Game Boy ouch!
Gliding with your Game Boy ouch!
Sliding off the sky scraper ouch!
Sliding all over the place ouch!

And this is the end of my life!

Stephen Clarke (9)
Roxeth Manor Middle School

THE STAFFROOM

What lurks behind the staffroom door
I bet you want to know
Is it nice or nasty, no one's sure
Where kids can never go.

Is it an alien spaceship
Or maybe it's a disco
Can my teacher do a backflip
I'd really like to know.

I know they eat and drink in there
I've heard them laugh and chat
They go there when they've time to spare
My friends and I know that.

Maybe it's dark and full of gloom
Do they keep a scary creature
How can I see that mystery room
I'll have to become a teacher.

Emma Carter (10)
Roxeth Manor Middle School

INSTRUMENTS

Kongos, Bongos
Don't use a beater
Because with your hands
It looks much neater.

Cabasas, maracas
Shake or roll
If you bang a bass drum
It will frighten your soul.

Triangles hit by angles
Makes a louder ding
That's our music lesson
Till the bell rings.

Joanna Stevens (11)
Roxeth Manor Middle School

GUESS WHO?

Ground walkers
Loud talkers
Mad shoppers
Crime stoppers.

Gum chewers
Coffee brewers
Office workers
Shadow lurkers.

Money spenders
Loan lenders
Book readers
Arguing leaders.

Music makers
Valuable takers
Chocolate eaters
Teaching teachers.

A life to live with to make us people!

Deepa Nair (11)
Roxeth Manor Middle School

THE BOYS IN OUR SCHOOL

Some boys are cute
And play the flute.

Most boys are cool
Some boys drool.

Boys always fart
But they think they're smart.

Boys act like kings
And can't even sing.

Boys annoy the teacher
And boys impress girls,
Especially the one's with golden curls.

Some boys are lovely
Some boys are ugly.

Marina Kapour (11)
Roxeth Manor Middle School

GUESS WHO?

Branch swinger.
Games player.
Group member.
Tree climber.
Forest home-maker.
Flea picker.
Puzzle solver.
Banana eater.
Expression maker.
Neighbourhood fighter.

Louise Allen (10)
Roxeth Manor Middle School

AUTUMN

Autumn rushed,
through the silent and dark creepy forest.
As he passed each tree he cracked each leaf
And branch with his enormous force.

Autumn made a huge and unbreathable breeze,
Lifting each broken and torn leaves with a swish
They would float and race through the forest
Until autumn cooled down with his fierce temper.

Autumn's temper,
Increases and with his powerful howling whip
Cracks and breaks each tree down.

Ibrahim Mughal (10)
Roxeth Manor Middle School

WHAT SHOULD I DO?

Each chocolate on the jar,
I spy one Milkybar.

One Milkybar sitting on the table,
I spy two juicy bagels.

Two juicy bagels on a plate,
I spy three big fat Jakes.

Three big fat Jakes eating the plates too,
I spy with my little brain what should I do?

Roshane Banbury (11)
Roxeth Manor Middle School

AUTUMN

Autumn is closed,
He's not very confident.
Autumn is a little boy,
Who feels like a thief.

He's not sure
How people are going to greet him.
He has taken
All of the Summer's glory.

Autumn jumps heavily,
Unlike Spring or Summer.
He wishes
That his father was here.

Autumn gets the feeling
That people don't like him.
Autumn persuades
The sun to come out
But it's just no use.

Now Autumn sulks,
Everywhere he goes.
People start to understand,
That Autumn also has feelings,
Likc every other person in the world.

It's the end
Of November
And his father, Winter
Is here.

Deepali Padharia (11)
Roxeth Manor Middle School

SEASONS

S ummer is the time of fun!
U mbrellas are not needed
M idsummer's Eve
M ost people go to the beach
E veryone has fun
R ainy days should not be seen.

S pring is the time for blossom
P eople pick some flowers
R oses are blooming
I can see the flowers in the meadow
N one of the trees should be bare
G ardens are filled with charming flowers.

W inter is a time for snow
I ice is slippery and cold
N ever ever ice skate on a frozen pond
T ime for throwing snowballs
E veryone sits near a warm fire
R efreshing the coldness outside.

A utumn is a time of falling leaves
U were playing in the fallen leaves
T ime for animals to find a home
U mbrellas are blown away
M ost of the leaves are bare
N ight is getting really cold.

Rajsana Rajendran (9)
Roxeth Manor Middle School

THE GHOST BY THE MOONLIGHT

In the most sombre corner of my garden,
Stands an elegant red rose on its own,
Which looked at the sunlight and gave a great sigh,
As her precious life was in the ghost's hand . . .

At moonlight he would come to dance with his bride,
And there she would weep her tears to the birds
                                    under the moon . . .

One day her happiness was back as she was picked for a
present on Valentine's Day.
Katie, named her Rose-Valentina
And Valentina the rose forgot the ghost,
But now I can still hear the sad howls of the ghost
                                    by the moonlight.

Kasthurie Murugesu (10)
Roxeth Manor Middle School

WINNIE THE POOH AND FRIENDS!

Winnie The Pooh is a bear.
His *best* friend Christopher Robin says 'Silly old bear.'
Tigger, Pooh Bear's old friend, always says, '*Hhhooooooooo*'
Piglet, his other friend, who is shy.
Then we come to Rabbit his bossy friend.
Then we get to Owl, a very clever friend.
Now we have Eeyore, a boring old fellow.
Roo and Kanga very nice fellows.
Now the best character
Is *Winnie The Pooh!*

Trisha Patel (10)
Roxeth Manor Middle School

WINNIE THE POOH

Winnie the Pooh and Christopher Robin having fun all the time,
Eeyore, Owl, Piglet and Tigger help make the honey,
After all the fun, Christopher makes money,
They all gather round and make more honey to eat.
All their lips get yellow and smell like honey,
There's . . .
Piglet who is so small,
Eeyore, who is so fat,
Tigger who is so popular he thinks,
Christopher who is a good friend.
And Winnie The Pooh is so cute and loves honey.
He is so light that he can float when he is swimming.
He is so *loveable!*
I love him so much so cuddly!

Sukhvinder Nandhra (10)
Roxeth Manor Middle School

I WONDER

There she sat
On the small wooden chair.
Drifting to a far off land.
A place where people are forgiving, caring and loving.
And a place where dreams have no end.
Was there really a land like this one?
Or was it all just her imagination?
The question still stands,
Is there really a land where the spirits come flying
In on their white feathered wings
And visit us every day?
A place filled with music and love?

Khyati Shah (11)
Roxeth Manor Middle School

THE NAUGHTIEST BOY IN SCHOOL

The naughtiest boy in school
Is the one who never listens at all
If he chatters and natters all day long
All his sums he will get wrong.

In the playground he is rough
He thinks that he is very tough
He's always thinking of other things
He stays outside when the school bell rings.

He ignores me in the playground every day
He never listens to what I say
But when we get home from school
He gives me a hug and everything's cool!

Alex Mahoney (10)
Roxeth Manor Middle School

THE WATERFALL

Blue and green and aquamarine.
Of all the things I could have seen
In all of the different places
In all of the different cases.
Down in London by Big Ben
I wouldn't give it ten out of ten.
The reason definitely being,
Of all the things I have been seeing,
Down by the greenish waterfall,
It's definitely best of all.

Niamh Ging (10)
Roxeth Manor Middle School

SAND, SAND

Sand, sand everywhere
Sand, sand in my hair
Sand, sand on my nose
Sand, sand between my toes.

Sand, sand in my shoes
Sand, sand all on you
Sand, sand in my short
Sand, sand on my note.

Sand, sand in my chocolate mousse
Sand, sand in my orange juice
Sand, sand on my hand
Everywhere is sand, sand.

Rimsha Chaudhry (10)
Roxeth Manor Middle School

SUN SHINES IN THE SKY

The sun shines brightly in the sky,
And the birds go flying by.
It's shining so children can go to the park,
Like a boy named Clark.
While the sun is shining by my last words are
Goodbye.

Karim Brown (9)
Roxeth Manor Middle School

THE SMALL GHOSTIE!

When it's late and it's dark
And everyone sleeps . . . shhh shhh shhh,
Into our kitchen
A small ghostie creeps . . . shhh shhh shhh.

We hear knocking and raps
And then rattles and taps,

Then he clatters and clangs
And he batters and bangs,

And he whistles and yowls
And he screeches and howls . . .

So we pull up our covers over our heads
And we block up our ears and
We stay in our beds!

Anam Khot (9)
Roxeth Manor Middle School

BEST FRIENDS

B   est friends you can trust
E   ver told secrets to a friend?
S   lept round a friend's house?
T   alk to a friend when you're lonely.

F   eel lucky with a friend?
R   eal friends stay together forever.
I   n school do you have fun with friends?
E   ver felt special with a friend?
N   ever leave a friend sad
D   o you feel special with a friend?
S   pecial friends mean a lot to you.

Chanelle Raj (10)
Roxeth Manor Middle School

ANIMAL ACTIONS

Down, down, down the creaky stairs,
Deep into the cave by the grizzly bears.
If you look up and stare with a torch,
You'll see that tiger out on the porch.
He'll bite you, he'll eat you, he'll grab you, who knows?
But he'll never smile, or give you a rose.

Then comes the lion, fierce and strong,
He'll do some things right, and some things wrong.
He bites with his teeth,
He scratches with his claws,
He walks around with his fancy paws.

Next come the bats hovering in the sky,
Swinging and swirling and never being shy.
Now these animals come to a rest
And now this poem closes, for the very, very best.

Alysha Ladha (10)
Roxeth Manor Middle School

HEDGEHOG

A fierce shell
A hurting hell

A small head
A leg of lead

A little late
A flat mate

A bonfire bed
A little dead

Lorelei Reason (10)
Roxeth Manor Middle School

DOG MEMORIES
(In Memory of Biggles 23.1.87 - 21.4.98)

We met it feels such a short time ago
You snapped at me unneedingly so
Yet despite your fears our happiness grew
And we discovered true friendship too.

I remember how we used to play
I recall those fun filled days
With crunchy treats and bouncy balls
And you would leap on me until I'd fall.

Goodbye may seem forever
But farewell is not the end
Because in my heart you will always be
My trusted and beloved friend.

Stephen Anderson (10)
Roxeth Manor Middle School

MY FRIEND

A secret sharer
A kind carer

A loyal chum
A pain in the bum!

A fab mate
A croissant crate

A purple lover
A real nutter!

(And my friend)

Tharanny Srisatkunam (11)
Roxeth Manor Middle School

PENGUIN

A fish stalker
A funny walker.

A good diver
A wave rider.

A fun player
A light weigher.

A water paddler
A loud babbler.

A rock tripper
A wing flipper.

A catalogue to make me
Penguin!

Penny Harandy (10)
Roxeth Manor Middle School

PEOPLE

Tall, small,
We all have a ball
Good, bad,
We're all sad
The teacher is glad
But sometimes she's mad
Short hair, long hair,
We're all fair
Blue eyes, brown eyes,
Can't you see my eyes.
Fat, thin,
Mind my chin.

Dawn Maidment (8)
Roxeth Manor Middle School

SEASON SONG

Here's a song
Stags give tongue
Winter snows
Summer goes
High cold blow
Sun is low
Brief his day
Seas give spray
Fern clumps redden
Shapes are hidden
Wild geese raise
Worried cries
Cold now grids
Wings of birds
Toy time
That's my time.

Nadia Farooqi (10)
Roxeth Manor Middle School

MONEY

I can't stop thinking about money,
My dad finds it funny.
He thinks I'm mad,
My mum thinks I'm sad.
I can't stop thinking about money.
I like to eat lots of honey,
My friend is just like me,
He is after some money.
I can't stop thinking about money.

Monica Mehta (9)
Roxeth Manor Middle School

TIGER

A good pouncer
A not so good bouncer

A very loud roarer
A quiet snorer

A long sleeper
A high leaper

A meat eater
A non hater

A pry hunter
A non grunter

A catalogue
To make me
Tiger

Jennifer Maidment (11)
Roxeth Manor Middle School

THE ONE BEFORE MY EYES

Her eyes are as deep as the blue ocean
Her lips are as red as the petals of the red roses.
When she smiles, the stars are ashamed to show their ugly faces.
Her teeth are as white pearls.
Her hair cannot be compared with any mortal.
The scent from her fine figure smells of fresh lavender.
When she walks the land behind her seems to be blessed.
She walks like a delicate deer.
Her body is as fragile as glass.
It appears to me as if she is the goddess of love.
She is my love.

Nikki Joshi (10)
Roxeth Manor Middle School

CATS

My favourite animals are cats
Cats are awfully popular,
If you have one be sure to
Have some mats.
They're related to the lion.

But they don't have as big a paw,
(as a lion) . . . and . . .
They don't have as big a roar
Only a miaow!

All the time cats wander round freely,
They're really, really pretty.
But, they don't look a bit
Like Cat Deeley!

Katherine Costello (9)
St Joseph's RC Junior School, Wembley

LIFE WITH COLOUR

Paint on the ceiling
Paint on the floor
Paint on the window
Paint on the door
Paint on the table
Paint on my chair
Paint on everything
Except on my paper
There's no paint on there.

Shakira Johnson-Thomas (10)
St Joseph's RC Junior School, Wembley

THE FUTURE

What will the future be like?
Will there be World War III?
Or will there be only a tree?
Will there be flying cars
Or only bleeding scars?
We can only find out in another 2000 years!

Romesh Navaratnasingham (10)
St Joseph's RC Junior School, Wembley

LUNCH

Oh! I have a hunch
Breakfast, dinner and lunch
Oh I would like to munch
A bowl of crunch
With a bunch of roses
Just for me.

Kane Falcao (10)
St Joseph's RC Junior School, Wembley

FOXES

Foxes come out at night
Often when you're asleep
He will creep into the light
And might have a bite to eat.

Shane Togher (10)
St Joseph's RC Junior School, Wembley

THE STARS

The stars are near Mars
Higher than cars
Brighter than light
A very small sight
Crystal light
If you are lost at night
You will see a very small light
The sky that is *bright!*

Jeffrey Sangalang (9)
St Joseph's RC Junior School, Wembley

THE BEST TEACHER

My teacher is as nice as a teddy bear
She has beautiful blonde hair
She gives you some sweets
If you're lucky some lovely treats
Miss, Miss, she's the best
Better than all the rest.

Roisin Finnerty (9)
St Joseph's RC Junior School, Wembley

THE DARK, DARK TREES

The dark, dark trees
Have lost their leaves
On the ground,
Where they can be found
You can see them high
While you say goodbye.

Shannon Cant (10)
St Joseph's RC Junior School, Wembley

MOTHER NATURE

Trees are light and dark green,
Every bit of grass is supreme,
Wood is brown,
The king wears a crown,
My swimming pool is blue,
I know there's a clue.

Robert Sumner (10)
St Joseph's RC Junior School, Wembley

I DON'T KNOW WHY?

I don't know why he stops and stares,
He looks at me as if he is saying something.
Telling me to do something.
He laughs at me,
And shouts out secrets,
He eavesdrops,
But I know I'll understand someday . . .

Monique Opeñano (9)
St Joseph's RC Junior School, Wembley

THE POWER OF FIRE

Fire glistens on a cold dark night
In a campsite.
Warming up freezing hands
But when there's a fire it goes all over the land.
Fire can cause to destroy a mill,
And it can also kill.

Brian Udokoro (10)
St Joseph's RC Junior School, Wembley

STARS

Stars, stars up in the sky
I wonder why?
Do they party all night long
Till the clock strikes one
Then rest for a while
And smile when they return.

Christopher Gunn (10)
St Joseph's RC Junior School, Wembley

FOOTBALL

My football team is called Junior Bess
When I got there my manager was drinking tea.

I said come on manager we've got some work to do
But he liked Pokêmon and thought of men.

I was playing football with my mates
They were eating chips
And this is a bad taste.

I hate school but I like football
And I always act cool.

I played football but I tripped over
And my mum went to bingo and
The man said 80 blind 80.

I like the book called 'Fire the Football'
Because it's a book for boys
and really hate playing with toys.

Callum Beharie (8)
St Lawrence RC Primary School, Feltham

HARRY POTTER

Harry Potter and his wizarding way
Always likes to have his say
With his arch enemy Draco Malfoy.

His house elf who tries to stop him
Coming to school.
He went to the barrier and came to a halt,
Because Dobby played a prank on him.

Dobby says Harry will be killed,
So when Harry plays Quidditch
Dobby puts a spell on the bludger and
Catches the snitch.

Harry's now thirteen in his third year
He trickles a tear because he gets his first
Birthday card that Hedwig,
Errol and Hogwart's owl delivered it to him.

That's Potter's review.

Hannah Lang (9)
St Lawrence RC Primary School, Feltham

FRIENDS

Friends are nice, sweet and always fun
If you hurt yourself they will help you.
If you have trouble spelling they will help you.
If you get knocked over they will help you.
Friends are always there to help you.
If someone is trying to come between you,
Don't let them.
Friends are always there to be your friend.

Sasha Nicholls (9)
St Lawrence RC Primary School, Feltham

BEST FRIENDS

Best friends are so great
Sometimes they forget about their mate
Some are tall, and some are small
Sometimes they're as tall as a wall.

They play with each other
And care for each other
And nothing can break them up.

When you get knocked over
Your best friend comes over
And when you sleep over
They steal the cover.

Best friends are very clever
They don't really say never
They listen to you when you're upset
Because they're as great as a pet.

Catherine Stoten (9)
St Lawrence RC Primary School, Feltham

FRIENDS

Friends arc people that help each other
And people that keep an eye on you.

We have lots of different kinds of friends
Some in school and some out of school.

Your brothers and sisters are your friends
Your parents are your friends and so is your family.

I go out with them at parties and during the day as well.

Rachel Dennehy (8)
St Lawrence RC Primary School, Feltham

MY NEW HOUSE

My new house will be shiny and new,
Some of the rooms may be painted bright blue.
The kitchen is big and full of steel
And the grass in the back garden is very real.

There's lots of places to play hide-and-seek,
I can't wait for the day to come when we move,
So I count the days every week.

There's lots of room for all our things,
And I can't wait for all the happiness
Our new house brings.

Annabelle Green-Terry (9)
St Lawrence RC Primary School, Feltham

THE GARDEN IS FULL OF WITCHES

Mum! The garden's full of witches
Come quick and see the witches
There's a full moon out
And they're flying about
Come on you'll miss the witches.

Mum there are witches in the garden.

Oh you'll miss the witches
They are dancing around our bridges
The witches are twitching at us.

Katie Robshaw (8)
St Lawrence RC Primary School, Feltham

SPORTS ARE FUN!

Every sport is fun,
Whenever I have a match I always have an iced bun.

Sports are fun,
I love it so much.

My hobby is being a footballer,
And when the ball is in the air I want to be a bit taller.

Sports are fun,
I love it so much.

I sometimes play cricket and it opens up my eyes,
And for my birthday I got a cricket surprise.

Sports are fun,
I love it so much.

My dad used to go to school and play rugby
And when I wanted to play I was amazed what he said to me.

Sports are fun
I love it so much.

I used to be good at golf but now I'm not,
And when I went to a football match it was quite fun.

Sports are fun,
I love it so much!

Michael Timbs (8)
St Lawrence RC Primary School, Feltham

IT WAS REALLY GREAT

There was a fish to be the swimming teacher,
and a lion to be the headmaster
and a gorilla to be the PE teacher.

It was really great! It was really cool
When the animals came to run our school.

We had a monkey to be caretaker
and a rabbit to do art.
A pig to be a teacher.

It was really great, it was really cool
When the animals came to run our school.

A duck to be a dinner lady
A chipmunk to be the cook
A cat to be a bin.

It was really great, it was really cool
When the animals came to run our school.

There is a tiger to keep off bullies
a tree frog to get apples off the tree
a flying gecko to be the deputy head.

It was really great, it was really cool
when the animals came to run our school.

Andrew Guidera (9)
St Lawrence RC Primary School, Feltham

THE DAY THE ANIMALS CAME TO RUN OUR SCHOOL

A monkey to be our head teacher,
A hyena to ring the bell
A koala to be the welfare.

It was really great!
It was really cool!
When the animals came to run our school!

A kangaroo for the sports teacher,
A cheetah for the caretaker,
A dog for a monitor.

It was really great!
It was really cool!
When the animals came to run our school!

A lion cleans the windows,
A tiger to play football,
A snake to be a book monitor.

Holly Riley (9)
St Lawrence RC Primary School, Feltham

CLOWNS

It must be fun to be a clown,
twisting, turning upside down.
Ever acting like a fool
Breaking every golden rule.
Chasing all our cares away
Bringing laughter to our day.
Bouncing and jumping every way,
People laughing every day.

Janet Blankson (8)
St Lawrence RC Primary School, Feltham

PARROTS WITH CARROTS

I was a little boy and I had a parrot
The doctor said this is a tropical parrot
and it only eats carrots.

I have a parrot
with lots of carrots.

I was walking down the supermarket
and my parrot spotted some carrots
So I went to see my friend's parrot
he was eating a carrot.

I have a parrot
with lots of carrots.

Haydn Lauder (8)
St Lawrence RC Primary School, Feltham

SCHOOL IS NICE

I think school is nice and brainy
But every time I go it is always rainy
I already took a bath
But I'd prefer to do maths
Every time I go to breaktime
I don't always get lemon and lime
At lunch time I like nice things to eat
Good thing they don't serve any meat
I think St Lawrence is good
I am in a nice happy mood.

Stevan Pavani (7)
St Lawrence RC Primary School, Feltham

I May Be Low But I Still Grow

I go to school
But Miss doesn't look down
So I make a sound.

I may be low but I still grow.

I go to get a book from the shelf
But I can't reach
I'm as small as an elf.

I may be low but I still grow.

I go to the shop
And get tangled up with a mop
But no one can see me.

I may be low but I still grow.

I go outside to play on a swing
But am too small so my mum puts me in.

I am low but I still grow.

Paige Nardone (9)
St Lawrence RC Primary School, Feltham

Laser Beam

I am a football player and my name is Nick,
I am a football player and I am very quick!

I am the captain of the team,
The team's name is Laser Beam!

I am a football player I get paid one thousand pounds,
I am a football player I win all my football rounds!

I am the captain of the team
The team's name is Laser Beam!

Connor Field (9)
St Lawrence RC Primary School, Feltham

MY DOG BLUE

I have a dog
His name is Blue,
Blue ran away
So I did too.

I ran after Blue,
Far, far away.
But then Blue stopped
So I said 'Hey!'

'I have been chasing you
All round the town,
So stop running now,
Or I'll take you to the pound.'

Blue looked upset,
So I rubbed his ears,
'Don't you ever, ever disappear!'

So I hugged Blue,
And Blue hugged me.
We're a happy family.

Daniella Lobo (9)
St Lawrence RC Primary School, Feltham

THE HUMMINGBIRD

I looked quite fine,
When I saw the sunshine.

It was shining bright,
With its fascinating light.

Then a rainbow appeared,
Because it heard,
The lovely sound of a hummingbird.

The bird sang a song,
To celebrate with *Hong Kong*

The sun and the rainbow said
'That song's cool
Can you teach us at school?'

Of course I would,
But you'd better be good.

Sing quite high,
Don't be shy,
I'll be proud if you try.

Nicole El-Baba (8)
St Lawrence RC Primary School, Feltham

BOOKS ARE COOL

Some books are cool!
Some books are dumb!
Some books will make you rub your tum.

Books are cool!
Books are fun!
Books are made for everyone.

Some books will rhyme!
Some books are mine!
Some books will take a long time.

Books are cool!
Books are fun!
Books are made for everyone.

Jessica-Rhae Bates (8)
St Lawrence RC Primary School, Feltham

TODAY IT IS MY BIRTHDAY

Today at 8.10pm it will be my birthday,
But it is only 7.00am I have to wait.
A long time, oh why?

Today it is my birthday!

Mum said it is time to go to school,
I said yes because it is Friday,
The last day of school!

Today it is my birthday!

Oops! I forgot I have to go to football lessons
After school,
And it lasts for two hours oh no!

Today it is my birthday!

At last it's my birthday countdown,
10, 9, 8, 7, 6, 5, 4, 3, 2, 1, 0 birthday party!

Samuel Addy (9)
St Lawrence RC Primary School, Feltham

I Am Low But I Will Grow

I am small so I cannot reach the door
But my mum or dad opens it so I can get
Out to my school at St Paul's.

I am low but I will grow!

When I go to school I cannot reach the desk
So the teacher has to give me a high chair
And everybody laughs at me.

I am low but I will grow!

When I go out with my mum to buy sweets
I cannot reach them
So my mum gets them.
She has to put them on the till.

I am low but I will grow!

When I have dinner with everyone I try
To sit on a big chair like everyone
But I fall off.

I am low but I will grow!

Every time on the way to the market with my dad
The cars don't see me and I nearly get run over.

I am low but I will grow!

Rachel Phippen (9)
St Lawrence RC Primary School, Feltham

I Am Low But I Will Grow

I cannot reach the doorknob
I cannot reach the corn on the cob
I need to get a stool because I am very small.

I am low but I will grow.

My dad hides the sweets up high so I cannot reach
So when I want them I just hold my head and screech.

I am low but I will grow.

I go out to the shops and line up in the queue
But no one ever notices me
They only notice you.

I am low but I will grow.

Everything is very high
Nearly up to the sky
I always go on my tipsy-toes
Everybody knows.

I am low but I will grow.

You are high and I am low
But that doesn't mean I won't grow.

I am low but I will grow.

Vivienne Marry (8)
St Lawrence RC Primary School, Feltham

BUT WE ARE STILL FRIENDS

I've got a small nose,
You've got a big nose,
I've got eight baby teeth,
You've got three baby teeth.

But we still are friends!

I've got short hair,
You've got long hair.
I am messy
You are tidy.

But we still are friends!

I've got brown hair
You've got blond hair.
My favourite colour is red,
Your favourite colour is pink.

But we still are friends!

But we are perfect friends!

Jessica Bryan (9)
St Lawrence RC Primary School, Feltham

BOOKS ARE COOL, BOOKS ARE FUN
BOOKS ARE MADE FOR EVERYONE

Books are made for me and you
So read a book.
The more you read the smarter you get
So read a book.

Books are cool
Books are fun
Books are made for everyone.

Some books are good some books are boring
I read the books to get me going.
Some books are long, some books are short,
I read the long books because they're just right for me.

Books are cool
Books are fun
Books are made for everyone.

James Cox (9)
St Lawrence RC Primary School, Feltham

THE BATH AND THE SEA

Bath water's hot
Seawater's cold
Bath water has bubbles
Seawater has foam
Bath water smells sweet of
Flowers, fruit or trees.
Seawater smells sour of
Seaweed, fish and sand.
Bath water is calm
Seawater's choppy.
There's a tidemark round
My bath it always stays the same
There's a tide mark on the beach,
But it never is the same.

Jane Owen (9)
St Lawrence RC Primary School, Feltham

I Have Too Many Pets

One pet, two pets I have
Too many pets.

I've got a cat, I've got a dog
And guess what else a fish and a hog.

One pet, two pets I have
Too many pets.

A rabbit
A snake
And a big fat pig.

One pet, two pets I have
Too many pets.

I've got a horse to play with
And a pony as well.
But sometimes I'm still so very lonely.

One pet, two pets I have
Too many pets.

A rat and
A gerbil
And two tiny mice.

One pet, two pets I have
Too many pets.

Loretta Bricknell (9)
St Lawrence RC Primary School, Feltham

HALLOWE'EN

Hallowe'en Hallowe'en
What a scary time
Hallowe'en Hallowe'en
A time witches are seen.

Hocus-Pocus
Toil and trouble
Mix your potion
Mildred Hubble.

Hallowe'en Hallowe'en
Spiders hide in attic corners
Hallowe'en Hallowe'en
Now the trick or treaters have been.

Abracadabra
Stir that potion
Mummies hide in the shade
Now my potion has been made.

Ghost and ghouls
With spooks to fool
Behold an eerie sight.

At last I can give you
A tremendous fright!

Rebecca Broad (9)
St Lawrence RC Primary School, Feltham

BABIES

I am a baby girl, I come from my mummy
I actually nearly burst from her tummy!
I can barely reach the table
and when I try to walk I trip up.

I can't walk so I have to crawl around the house
until I can learn how to walk and how to talk.
I am very low but I hope I will grow.
I just grow very slow.

When I am bigger I will get to go to school.
I think going to school will be really really cool.
I will make lots of friends but this all depends on if I ever grow.

Shannon McBride (9)
St Lawrence RC Primary School, Feltham

I'M AN ANT

I'm an ant, very small,
It makes me wonder why I'm not tall.
I feel like a dot in a big, big world,
So I still wonder why I am small.

I do not grow not even slow,
And so I wonder why I don't grow.
Why don't I grow?

Why am I here, what is my purpose,
Why do I just crawl around on the surface.
I'm an ant.

Thomas Clark (9)
St Lawrence RC Primary School, Feltham

SUPERMAN SAM

Superman Sam
Saving people in distress
Superman Sam
He wears his pants over his dress
Superman Sam
He plays his PlayStation all night
With the baddies he always gets in a fight
With his bright red leotard and his Super Sam cape,
He gets interviewed over a tape
Superman Sam gets shot without blood,
Superman Sam saves people from floods,
After a brawl or a fight,
He still asks his mum to tuck him in at night.

Charles Pansoy Cunniff (10)
Victoria Junior School

BART AND HOMER SIMPSON

Bart and Homer went to the shops and they saw a clown
But before they said anything he gave them a frown.

Homer saw something and said 'Quick Bart look over there.'
So Bart sharply turned and he saw a bright green pear.

Bart hesitated and said 'Er . . . Homer can I have a car'
'No son, you can't but let's have a drink at Moe's bar.'

Homer and Bart had a long day so Homer went to bed
And Bart tucked Homer in but Homer fell and cracked his head.

Chris Hunt (11)
Victoria Junior School

INDIA

A rickshaw man rides by,
With rich women
Whose scarves are so high, that they almost fly.

Fiery-hot, reds, oranges and yellows
Colour the markets
Where sellers shout and bellow.

Spices fill our noses,
The curry dishes smell hot and spicy
Then in the garden we smell our neighbour's roses.

Gold, silver, bronze ornaments and pictures of gods everywhere.

Tasty food, smells, tasty flavour and burning hot.

Big houses look shiny with the smell of rice and chapaties
You can see chubby women walking outside,
Smelling the lovely food
At the end the rich women get off the rickshaw.

Neetu Dhillon (7)
Victoria Junior School

FOOTBALL

Football is class
Only if you pass
It is a laugh
After playing you'll need a bath.

I love to play football
Even though I'm very small
I am a girl who likes her sports
I wish I owned a sports court.

I like to play football all the time
If I do bad it's like a crime,
I am a girl who likes her sports,
All the time, every day.

I am a top sporty girl
I'm not like those other girls that do twirls.
I am different from the rest
But I know football's the best.

Samantha Oña (10)
Victoria Junior School

THERE WAS A MAN FROM FELTHAM

There was a man from Feltham
He was singing so loud
And he was so proud
He got into the singles
And ate 2000 pringles,
And felt terribly sick,
And found a big massive stick,
There was a man from Feltham.

There was a man from Feltham
He liked to do some swimming
And a bit of skimming
There was a man from Feltham.

There was a man from Feltham
He wore a skirt,
And didn't like shirts,
There was a man from Feltham.

Kaylie Tompkins (9)
Victoria Junior School

BART SIMPSON THE LITTLE DEVIL

Bart Simpson is really cool,
But sometimes he acts like a fool,
Bart Simpson is really cool,
He really, really raps and rules.

Bart Simpson has a dad,
But he says, 'Bart my lad
Go and get me some beer from the fridge.

Go on Bart you little midge.'

He lays on the sofa eating, drinking,
And as he lays on the sofa
Always sinking.

Bart sits on the sofa
Watching Itchy and Scratchy,
He wears an orange top
Which is very catchy.

Well let's just say Bart Simpson is a devil
Let's hope we don't get to be on his level.

Jasmine Bailey (10)
Victoria Junior School

WILLIAM BEECH

William Beech is a skinny thing,
He only wishes he could sing
He has no friends to play with,
But Tom has bought a paint kit.

When he shows Tom the scars,
They looked red like Mars.
William moved to the country,
And had to live with Tom Oakley.

William was a bit frightened,
And Tom got very tightened,
He is only eight,
And has a mate.

Leah Arnold (10)
Victoria Junior School

WILLIE BEECH

Willie Beech is very lonely
And his body looks very bony
He is battered and bruised by his mum
Who has made his childhood lack any fun
She doesn't treat him like her son.

Now he is an evacuee
He is with Mr Tom Oakley
Mr Tom treats him very good
And that's the way his mum should.

Now he is fat not so skinny
He has a friend called Zackcry
He is dirty and smelly
And his belly used to be empty.

He likes Mr Tom better
And his mum hasn't sent a letter
If he could read and write
He would do it every night.
He's in safe hands
And he's in a safe land.
If he was in the same place
He would see the war
When he walked out the door.

Ali Belgiad (10)
Victoria Junior School

HIPPOGRIFF

A Hippogriff is half-horse half-eagle,
It is much bigger than a seagull,
You have to try and gain his trust,
Otherwise his claws he will thrust.

You have to bend and bow,
You cannot blink I don't know how,
If he bows too,
It means he likes you.

Then he will lower his wing,
And over his back your leg will fling,
Then he will fly up in the air,
Higher than a ten foot bear.

The Hippogriff is a magical creature,
His wings are a beautiful feature,
He has a lovely swishing tail,
He can fly through even hail,
He is a Hippogriff.

Craig Carman (11)
Victoria Junior School

BART SIMPSON

Bart Simpson is his name,
And trouble is his game.
He's really, really dumb,
And sometimes sticks out his bum!

Bart Simpson is good at sports,
This is his phrase 'Eat my shorts!'
When he sees his two aunts which are dumber,
He goes 'Aye Kurumba!'

Bart Simpson steals Homer's money,
And he just loves a juicy gummy.
He also wears his lucky red hat,
To keep him out of fights and that.

Bart Simpson is ten years old,
And he's not really bold.
So Bart Simpson is his name,
And trouble is his game.

Zaman Quyyum (10)
Victoria Junior School

THE BLUE PIG

There is a blue pig that helped little boys,
He gets fairies to give food and toys.
The little boys say 'Thank you Mr Pig,'
Then he disappears dancing the Irish jig.

He then goes and helps the little girls,
By giving them rubies and pearls.
The little girls say 'Thank you Mr Pig,'
Then he disappears dancing the Irish jig.

The blue pig goes and helps the old,
By giving them silver and gold.
The old say 'Thank you Mr Pig,'
Then he disappears dancing the Irish jig.

He then tried to help a hungry mole,
But he ate the poor piggy whole.
The mole said 'Thank you Mr Pig,'
But the blue pig was inside the mole
Dancing the Irish jig.

Sam Parker (10)
Victoria Junior School

THE MONSTER UNDER MY BED

He is really scary
And also hairy
Knock down a brick wall
And a shopping mall.

He has a big belly
The size of a big screen telly
We are very good friends
When he sleeps he pretends.

He is a really big dude
He likes to eat his food
He is funny
He has no money.

I go under my bed and play with him
He has a missing limb
I like him very much
He doesn't speak Dutch.

Lisa Gallagher (10)
Victoria Junior School

SUPERMAN WHO RAN

Superman who ran,
Came to see if there was trouble,
He saw a lady screaming,
She was in a painful muddle.

He tried to help her,
He really, really tried,
There was no one to help him,
So in the end he cried.

He pulled and pulled,
Until she was bleeding,
She wasn't enjoying this,
It's her mother she was needing.

Superman who ran,
Is not very strong,
Don't believe what he says,
He's very very wrong.

Sonnah Allte (10)
Victoria Junior School

WITCHES

Witches are very scary
And also very lary
They have got a big nose
And a broomstick like a hose.

People see them at night
And give people a big fright.
People hate them very much
And also can speak very good Dutch.

They eat frogs and toads
Along the road
And gobble them up
In their gut.

When they go to sleep
You don't hear a peep.
All night they snore,
And they fall on the floor.

Sarah Meades (10)
Victoria Junior School

OUTSIDE MY BEDROOM WINDOW

Outside my bedroom window,
Lie some scattering trees,
I used to think they were monsters,
Especially when the door creaks.

I would hear a bang, bang on the door,
And a clash, clash on the floor,
When the covers are over me,
My heart pounds, bleep, bleep.

When I need the loo,
I slowly walk out of my bed,
I look straight forward,
To stop me from banging my head.

I pull down my pyjama trousers,
To see a woman wearing big blouses.
She screeches and groans,
It makes me wobble my skinny bones.

I go back to my room,
I lie down on the windowpane,
I crash down on a flower pot
What a terrible pain.

It's morning I'm so tired
I feel like I've been fired.
I hear a bang, bang on the door,
And a little creak, creak on the floor.

Louise Osei-Kissi (10)
Victoria Junior School

THE TV

As they sit me on this stand
And sit down to watch me wobble.
While they hide my horrid hair,
My ears wide and fat.
They leave me here to sweat and stare.
They talk while poking me hard,
My chest aches from all the food,
They think I have no feelings but I do.
They can't hear my thoughts
I know they want me to die
They try and try but no time worked,
I see all my other friends
Being hurt and hit.

Wesley Jackson (10)
Victoria Junior School

BART SIMPSON

He acts if he is all cool,
Everyone calls him a fool.
He goes home
To play with Homer's foam.

He is America's bad boy,
And plays with his Krusty toy.
He stays at home staying cool
He hates school.

His phrase is 'Eat my shorts'
He doesn't do what his thought sport.
Bart Simpson's sister is Lisa,
She is a pain, he thinks she's insane.

Tom Lloyd (11)
Victoria Junior School

WILLIAM BEECH

Willie thinks he will go to Hell
But he is doing rather well.
When he came he was very smelly
Now he has a very full belly.
He was sent to Tom Oakley
Who lived locally.
He could not read or write
Going to school would be a fright.
At London in his home
His mum gave him not a bone.
He is as skinny as a pole
And dressed like a rag doll.
Willie and Zac, his mates
In school had to write on slates.
Willie doesn't know what is a torch
Tom told him as they sat on the porch.
Willie had muddy hair
When it was washed it turned the colour
of a mouldy pear.

Jenny Peaty (10)
Victoria Junior School

BART SIMPSON

Bart is a dude
But is always rude.
He is very funny,
But he hates honey.

Bart likes skateboards,
And sometimes thinks and hoards.
His hero is Krusty
But his room is dusty.

Bart has a sister
Who always gets caught up in a twister.
He has a dad who is fat,
And also has a dead pet bat.

Bart is cool,
But is not good in school.
His mum has big blue hair,
Which is quite rare.

Nikesh Pankhania (11)
Victoria Junior School

BART SIMPSON

Bart is so cool,
If you don't think so you're a fool.

When he was four,
He got in trouble with the law.

He don't like school,
But loves shopping at the mall.

His favourite phrase
Is 'Eat my shorts.!'

But then again he's very short.

His dad drinks beer
And has no fear.

He has a friend called Milhouse
Who brought a game called Thrill House.

He's very dumb,
And likes chewing gum.

Chloe-Lee Fitzwater (11)
Victoria Junior School

TRAMP

There is this person in my street
Who has dirty feet
They are as black as coal
And his shoes are not whole.

He is as thin as a blade,
And he always wears these cool blue shades.
He doesn't eat at all, only out of a bin,
And in his lifetime only had one gin.

There is this person in my street
Who is very sweet.
He also wears anything he gets
And also he does not bet.

There is this person in my street
Who has dirty feet.

Samantha Hendley (11)
Victoria Junior School

MOON

The moon is calm,
Like the sea,
Come and fly to the moon with me.
You'll meet the stars,
Right next to Mars.
They'll be your friend,
Right to the end.
It's time to go,
Goodbye my friend,
See you soon,
Again and again.

Leanne Eshet (10)
Wood End Park Community School

THE BEACH

The sea swooshes over the rocks,
The banana boat washes salty water in your mouth.
Waves crash across the orangey sand making it wet.
Adults and children play and mess around.
People hire boats with slides for their children.
Men and women surf and windsurf, most of the time they fall off.
Seaweed and sand at the bottom.
Beach balls thrown into the air.
Seagulls fly around.
Fishes, dolphins, sharks and other water and sand animals
have the pleasure of living in the
        Deep blue sea.

Cherelle Smith (11)
Wood End Park Community School

BUBBLE

Twirling transparent
Reflecting
The balls
Afloat.

Sphere
Sparking in
The moonlight
Sky glistening.

Round round
Amazing to
The last star.

Kieran Brewster (10)
Wood End Park Community School

BUBBLES

Glassing sphere gleaming
In the sky
Pop!

A shining star
Glistening on
The summer's day
Pop!

Popping
Reflecting, reflecting
Pop!

Changing to
Different shapes
Floating
Pop!

Pop, pop, pop
Pop!

Ashleigh Jeffs (11)
Wood End Park Community School

BUBBLE

Shining sphere
Shimmering in the sunlight
An amazing ball
Glittering in the
Summer's night
Floating

Down
Down
Bouncing off the table
Floating down
Down
Pop!

Simranjeet Kalyan (11)
Wood End Park Community School

BUBBLES

Floating sphere
Falling in the air
A glistening ball
Glowing in the sunshine.
Hotness.

Flying
Fall
Fall
Bouncing
To the table
Popping
Pop
Pop
Pop
P

o

p

Adam Burns (10)
Wood End Park Community School

BUBBLE

Floating ping-pong ball
Stalking the skies.

A glistening rainbow
Sparkling in the
Winter's frost.

Drowning slowly
Slowly
Spearheading to the ground.

Fading . . .
Pop . . .
Pop . . .
Pop . . .
P

o

p

Sandra Mall (10)
Wood End Park Community School

LITTLE MISS MUFFET . . . REVISED

Little Miss Muffet sat on a tuffet
Eating some Irish stew,
Along came a spider
Who sat down beside her
And she ate the spider too!

Christopher Woodside (11)
Wood End Park Community School

BUBBLES

Floating ball
Flying through the air
A spinning sphere.

Gliding down
To the ground
Falling
Slowly
Slowly.

Down
To the last drip
Down
To the last drip.
P

o

p

Vickie Flynn (10)
Wood End Park Community School